the ***essential***
GUIDE TO WORKPLACE MEDIATION & CONFLICT RESOLUTION

the *essential* GUIDE TO WORKPLACE MEDIATION & CONFLICT RESOLUTION

Rebuilding Working Relationships

Nora Doherty & Marcelas Guyler

KOGAN
PAGE

London and Philadelphia

First published in Great Britain and the United States in 2008 by Kogan Page Limited.

120 Pentonville Road
London N1 9JN
United Kingdom
www.koganpage.com

525 South 4th Street, #241
Philadelphia PA 19147
USA

ISBN 978 0 7494 5019 9

British Library Cataloguing-in-Publication Data

A CIP record for this book is available from the British Library.

Library of Congress Cataloging-in-Publication Data
Doherty, Nora.
  The essential guide to workplace mediation and conflict resolution : rebuilding working relationships / Nora Doherty and Marcelas Guyler.
      p. cm.
  Includes bibliographical references and index.
  ISBN 978-0-7494-5019-9
  1. Mediation and conciliation, Industrial. 2. Conflict management. I. Guyler, Marcelas. II. Title.
  HD5481.D57 2008
  658.3'145--dc22
                                        2007047479

Typeset by Saxon Graphics Ltd, Derby
Printed and bound in India by Replika Press Pvt Ltd

Contents

Preface

It has been quite an experience for us to be involved in the impetus and expansion in workplace mediation over the last 10 years or more. It appears, however, that the learning resources to back up this rapid growth have not kept pace. There are still limited practical books or resources on this subject.

One evening – after an intensive residential mediation training course – we were sat by a lake at the Hayes Conference Centre in beautiful Derbyshire and there and then we decided it was time someone wrote a book about workplace mediation that would provide the 'essentials' on the subject together with useful practical information, backed by real case studies and showing how organizations can integrate mediation into their practice, policies and work culture – and three years later here it is.

We were both working full time with our respective consultancy businesses so this book had to be written in short bursts on the odd occasions that we managed to get some spare time as we travelled around the UK. It is certainly a collaborative effort with some chapters written individually and some together – integrating our ideas and perspectives in the final chapter.

This book is about the 'essentials' of workplace mediation and conflict resolution for organizations and managers and is based on our own direct experience. There are many mediators out there with their own knowledge and practice of mediation. This book is *our* sharing of practical mediation experience, theories and typical case studies. Although we are not academics, we do offer in this book some useful models that we have created ourselves or have adapted from other sources. Central to our exposition is a model of workplace mediation based on a clear six-step structure, which is problem solving, transformative and ultimately empowering for all those taking part.

We bring to this venture both different and complementary experience and skills.

Nora Doherty (BA, MSc) has a background in psychotherapy, group work and communications skills training. She has been one of the UK's leading independent consultants in the field of workplace mediation for businesses and organizations and has been a mediator and trainer for many years. In 1998 she designed and created the first UK specialist accredited course to professionally train people to be workplace mediators, and she continues to offer these courses, and independent mediation, through her mediation consultancy company Professional Mediation Resolutions (PMR) Ltd.

Nora's working model of mediation – which she calls the 'six-step structure of mediation' – has been adopted by many in the field and she has also produced a workplace mediation video and DVD. She has personally carried out a huge number of successful mediations for individuals and teams, including complex cases of bullying and harassment.

Nora has particular interest in the emotional and relationship aspects of 'why relationships in the workplace break down' and in the part that mediation can play in re-building them again so that they are respectful, fair and sustainable. She also has an enduring interest in the spiritual dimension and in the practice of mindful meditation techniques that she sees as underpinning and sustaining her work within the field of resolving complex interpersonal conflict.

Marcelas Guyler (BA, PGCE and Master Practitioner of NeuroLinguistic Programming (NLP)) brings to this book business and organizational perspectives on conflict resolution from his career as a business trainer, communications and development consultant, workplace mediator and as Managing Director of The Human Business (THB) Limited, which was created in 2000 to deliver national Employee Assistance Programmes (EAPs) in the UK. THB has offered a wide range of employee and organizational supports that include employee counselling and individual and team mediations in support of conflict resolution.

Central to his work has been a fascination with process and a belief in the capacity of individuals and teams to evolve, to create and to self-empower when released from the constraints of restrictive organizational thinking or unquestioned personal self-limitation. Marcelas is now semi-retired and divides his time between his work in the UK, as principal consultant of MCRG (the Mediated Cultures and Resolutions Group), and his writing when based abroad.

'New figures from the CIPD's "Managing Conflict at Work" survey – of 1,190 employers – suggest that dealing with conflict is taking up more and more HR time. Over 60 per cent of respondents say they have seen an increase in the use of HR departments to resolve individual disputes in the past 12 months. And it is time-consuming and costly: employers say they are spending an average of 10.5 days per case dealing with disciplinary and grievance issues – little less than the 12.5 days they say is spent preparing for a tribunal case.'

Chartered Institute of Personnel and Development (CIPD) – *Managing Conflict at Work*

'On 1st October 2004, a new statutory minimum disciplinary and grievance procedure came into force as part of a government drive to ease the burden on the tribunal system and encourage employers to deal with their own disputes. But since most leading employers will already have these formal procedures in place, best practice is now more geared towards alternative dispute resolution.'

CIPD

'It was found that even the most intractable, longstanding and deeply emotive disputes benefited from mediation.'

ACAS research 2005

'The 2004 Regulations... have failed to produce the desired Policy outcome.... The key message from this review is that inflexible, restrictive regulation has been unsuccessful in this context.... I would like to comment on how employment disputes not solved in the workplace should be resolved in the future. My vision is of a greatly increased role for mediation.... Encouraged by signs of success in the context of employment disputes elsewhere in the world, I commend increased use of mediation to employers, employees and practitioners in Great Britain.'

Michael Gibbons – Foreword to the DTI *Better Dispute Resolution* report March 2007

'Put the key of despair into the lock of apathy. Turn the knob of mediocrity slowly and open the gates of despondency – welcome to a day in the average office.'

David Brent – from BBC sitcom *The Office*

Introduction

This book deals with the core concepts of workplace mediation and of conflict resolution for organizations and managers. It is written firstly for those people in organizations who are in the front line and who have daily to anticipate, pre-empt or defuse conflicts in the support of performance or the preservation of productive working relationships. It is also written for those who are already mediators or who are training to become mediators.

In writing this essential guide our intention has been to create a book that will prove valuable to public or private companies and to organizations worldwide. We have in mind therefore those in organizational development or in senior management who are concerned to systematize their approach to informal dispute resolution of grievances and complaints and who are responsible for deciding how conflicts are dealt with overall within the work culture.

It is a book that we hope will appeal not only to individuals who are interested in how to put mediation into everyday practice, but also to managers, human resource departments and ultimately those responsible for corporate or organizational strategy and grievance or conflict resolution policies.

WHY SHOULD I FIND OUT ABOUT WORKPLACE MEDIATION?

The simple answer we suggest is that there is a direct ratio between the quality of relationships across the workplace and long-term business effectiveness and success. This is a bold claim and calls for some explanation.

There is no denying in the short term that it is possible to drive an enterprise through aggressive management and economic dominance, even to the detriment of employees, customers or shareholders. Contemporary shock/horror stories about such ruthless tactics regularly appear in the business pages.

The claim that we make in this book is that power and control-driven business successes, though possible (and currently normative in 'dog eat dog' businesses or in hierarchical work cultures), are actually, in the longer term, neither sustainable nor essentially productive in human or financial terms.

In saying this, we are raising the curtain on the crucial alternative of the 'win–win' dynamic that is central to the power and success of mediation and that we will claim could be widely employed both in the pursuit of business profitability and success and in the motivation and empowerment of employees. We shall be exploring this possibility in greater detail as we reflect upon the nature, benefits and wider cultural applications of mediation.

Sadly, in everyday life, it is often the win–lose dynamic that holds sway and that drives so much of our contemporary workplace, social, judicial and political life. In our view, it is axiomatic that for every employee, shareholder, customer or voter who is hoodwinked into the surrender of their real interests, a victim is created who will at some point transform into an unintended enemy displaying a disconcerting desire for compensation or for punitive revenge.

In the long term, then, we claim that it is not power or control but the soundness of workplace, business and commercial relationships that underpin the long-term success of an enterprise. The central and lasting importance of mediation is that it addresses head-on the business of creating and restoring respectful workplace relationships. Mediation does this in a way that is fair, mutual and even-handed to all stakeholders involved.

Moreover, mediation involves a democratic and empowering process that is driven by, owned by and dependent for its success upon the involvement and creativity of the participants who elect to engage with this chosen solution. In a word, mediation gets straight to the heart of the matter by treating workplace relationships and employee involvement as key to conflict resolution. Mediation, in its wider cultural extension, is also central to the enhancement of workplace well-being, cooperation and productivity.

Whilst addressing the breakdown of workplace relationships, mediation also offers interesting new models and tools for enhancing communications and negotiation at all levels of management, as well as improving the quality of client or customer relationships and complaint handling.

Finally, mediation suggests cooperative and consensus models that offer challenging new business and commercial values and practices in the wider context of productivity and the cultural health of our organizations.

This book is directed therefore to anyone for whom this unique conflict resolution method and performance enhancement tool will prove both productive and cost effective – whether in terms of people, performance, finance, employee morale or ethical fairness and corporate soundness of values.

FINDING YOUR WAY AROUND THIS BOOK

This book comes in three main sections: Part I, Workplace mediation, considers what mediation is, why it is necessary, how it works, including its main principles of operation and the six-step structure of a mediation meeting. We also include in this first part a discussion of how to approach and carry out a team mediation when groups, teams or departments are experiencing difficulties.

Part II, Mediation in action, gives practical examples of typical workplace mediations for employees, managers, teams and directors. In this section, the authors have amalgamated and synthesized their individual and joint experiences of carrying out mediations for interpersonal disputes and complaints over their many years of being professional mediation consultants.

In Part III, In support of conflict managers, we examine why conflicts arise in the workplace and offer innovative and highly useful everyday conflict resolution communication skills for managers, including skills to defuse anger or aggression and the flexible Brief Mediation™ model for anyone who manages people and needs a speedy and effective way of resolving differences between staff or with customers. This section then expands into a review of new and emerging organizational models, the business of empowerment, and the way we view the culture and processes of mediation from the perspective of organizational development. The authors look to explore this argument against the background of the contemporary search for involvement, accountability and the 'can-do' flexibility so urgently needed to match up to the demands of contemporary business survival and organizational effectiveness.

Each chapter of the book ends with 'The essentials', which describes in brief the chapter content.

We hope you enjoy the book.

Introduction: the essentials

There is a direct ratio between the quality of relationships across the workplace and long-term business effectiveness and success. This book is about how mediation addresses these complex relationship difficulties head-on, so that respectful working relations can be restored for the long-term good of both employees and employers.

The book will be helpful to mediators, interested individuals and managers, and to organizations that are considering bringing mediation into their work culture, practices and policies.

PART I

Workplace mediation

In Part I we shall first examine the unique tool for conflict resolution that is 'workplace mediation': what it is, how it works and the special nature of its role and value within the continuum of conflict resolution interventions.

We shall then consider how mediation can be used within organizations, how it can address the needs of team and group conflicts and how mediation can be best introduced into your workplace culture, policy and practice.

1

So what exactly is workplace mediation?

At the outset we need to understand both the special nature and the underlying principles of workplace mediation. Following the theoretical groundwork in this chapter, we will go on to look at an example of workplace conflict in Chapter 2 and then, in Chapter 3, examine a practical six-step model that describes in detail the structure of mediation.

A WORKING DEFINITION OF MEDIATION

Initially, then, we will begin with a working definition of workplace mediation as a good starting place to get to grips with this new area of thinking and practice.

A definition of workplace mediation is as follows:
Mediation is a structured process whereby an impartial mediator facilitates communication between those in dispute in order for them to understand each other better and for them to come up with mutually acceptable solutions that will improve the working relationship in the future.

Nora Doherty, Managing Director, PMR Ltd

The skills of a mediator

Active listening and attention

Giving people space and safety to say what they need to say, giving good-quality attention and asking appropriate, encouraging questions of all parties in a fair and equal way.

Summarizing

Being able to remember and re-present key facts and issues in a non-blame, non-inflammatory way.

Building rapport

Creating an atmosphere of trust and safety, helping people feel that their thoughts and feelings are important and understood, giving them the chance to make their own decisions at their own pace, demonstrating a sincere interest in helping parties to resolve their differences.

Facilitation

Helping people to communicate and listen to each other, allowing appropriate, non-damaging expression of feelings, keeping the overall focus and direction of the mediation.

Impartiality

Remaining non-judgemental, impartial and fair throughout, giving equal attention and time to each person. Remaining professional and impartial – not taking sides.

Problem solving

Helping parties clarify the main issues that can be tackled in the mediation and encouraging them to explore and agree on win–win solutions, changes of behaviour or work practices, and strategies for action. Keeping the process positive and affirming, with an emphasis on how they would like things to be in the future.

Conflict management

Staying calm and assertive, and encouraging communication even when feelings are running high. Defusing anger and damaging, or overly negative feelings or attack. Keeping on track, keeping to what is most constructive for all involved.

Looking at the key concepts in the definition, we can immediately understand the purpose and indeed some of the clear advantages of using mediation to address conflict and the breakdown of workplace relationships. We shall examine this by unpacking the definition in its constituent parts.

'Mediation is a structured process'

Firstly, there is nothing haphazard about mediation. It is a structured and staged process that is clearly designed to facilitate and direct people from A to B, from deeply felt negatives of conflict to new agreed outcomes and constructive changes. Point 'A' – the outset – comprises whatever emerges as the starting place: the 'positions', problems or obstacles described by those in the conflict or the dispute. Point 'B' – the destination – is reached with the sign-up of mutually agreed proposals (the mediation agreements) that will restore or repair the working relationship.

It is the structure of the six steps of mediation that directs this journey and enables a resolution.

'Whereby an impartial mediator...'

At the centre of the mediation is the mediator who is witness to, and offers a process based upon, the underlying principle of 'impartiality'. In essence, this impartiality signifies a non-judgemental acceptance of people that is demonstrated in the mediator's even-handed attention, in equal respect for the participants and in validation of the participants' positive intention to find viable solutions to their problems. Mediators receive extensive training in how to remain impartial, how not to allow any biases or stereotyping to affect their behaviour, and how to avoid taking sides even when being challenged to do so.

'[A mediator] facilitates communication between those in dispute...'

Facilitated communication is the prime tool of mediation and forms the first dynamic employed by the mediator in the process. The early stages of mediation depend upon the careful unpacking of the perceptions and feelings of participants as to their conflict and their resulting experiences.

If you have ever been close to protracted workplace disputes you may think that by this point people will have already done a lot of 'communicating' – involving multiple accusations and much rehearsing with other people of their grievances and dissatisfactions. This is often true, but such accusations, grievances and outpourings of blame and complaints have actually nothing to do with the facilitated communication that forms the first process and concern of mediation.

'Communication' in the context of mediation is actually about enabling a quality of listening and the safe exchange of thoughts, feelings and information necessary to all parties in the mediation. This is important, as often communication by this point has completely broken down and the parties may not even be talking to each other. Mediation offers a safe place and safe ways with which to re-establish contact and to begin to listen fruitfully to each other.

'In order for them [the participants] to understand each other better...'

At this first stage of the mediation, the mediator seeks to ensure that people are able to express and listen to each other's perceptions, issues, needs and feelings. When this is done well, it can, not surprisingly, turn out to be a revelation to all those concerned. There can be a lot of misunderstandings and mis-assumptions on both sides.

What emerges from a skilfully facilitated mediation exchange is in fact a 'world away' from the accusations and rehearsed grievances that are normally associated with the hurtful or defensive exchanges of those stuck in conflict.

'The map is not the territory...' and what emerges throughout the mediation, in most mediators' experience, may bear little resemblance to the participants' first stated positions or their perceptions either of what has happened or what they feel the other person is 'doing to them'.

'And for them to come up with mutually acceptable solutions...'

If dynamic number one is about facilitated communication in the process of mediation, then dynamic number two is all about 'solutions' and a way forward.

The power for change inherent in any mediation is twofold: firstly there must be the initial willingness by the participants to search for solutions. This commitment forms the prime contribution that the participants themselves make to the success of the whole process.

The second powerful dynamic is introduced by the mediator and involves a 'future-based orientation' whereby the participants, having understood something about each other's experience and needs, are helped to explore their ideal future scenario, on the basis of which they can begin to build a mutually acceptable agreement that better suits their needs.

'Solutions that will improve the working relationship in the future.'

With this last line of the definition, we are back again at the starting point. The intention both at the outset and the end point of mediation remains the same: namely the improvement of workplace relationships. As such, mediation is, at the same time, both 'employee and performance led' and is actively directed towards this end by a skilled mediator.

Whilst we have covered the 'definition' of mediation above, underlying the nature and the practice of mediation are a number of guiding principles that support it. These principles have also a wider significance relevant to the conduct and ethics of business and workplace relationships, which will be considered especially in the final chapter of the book.

Before investigating the actual 'six-step structure' of mediation, which we will do in Chapter 3, we shall first review the main, classic principles that govern mediation as a specific dispute resolution method.

THE UNDERLYING PRINCIPLES OF MEDIATION

Underlying any activity are the informing principles that ensure both consistency and sound results. Mediation is not just an ad hoc meeting and not just any method of dispute resolution. It is based upon a number of commonly accepted principles. In other words, mediation is a specific dispute resolution method with its own set of operational principles.

These principles are particularly important when crucial boundaries are at risk or when developments threaten to directly sabotage the successful outcome. The elements described below are the main key

The main principles of mediation

▌ It is voluntary – all parties need to agree to mediation.
▌ It is solution/agreement focused.
▌ Parties offer the solutions themselves.
▌ The mediator is impartial and does not take sides.
▌ It is confidential.
▌ If mediation is unsuccessful, formal or legal procedures can be invoked.

principles or conditions that underpin the model and that may be said to distinguish mediation as a specific dispute resolution method.

Mediation is voluntary

In order for mediation to work, it is important that all concerned understand and agree that it is a voluntary process.

Mediation is unique in that, although the process is clearly directed and facilitated by the mediator, it is the *participants themselves who control* both the outcome and the mediated agreements. This participant *control* or *empowerment* operates from the outset – in that mediation cannot even take place without the agreement of each person to participate. Equally the early disclosure and clarification of the participants' issues cannot happen without a willingness to talk, to listen and to understand each other's agendas, issues and needs.

Finally, empowerment proceeds from the fact that solutions do not come from the mediator, nor from an imposed business solution but rather from the mutual agreement of the participants themselves. This voluntary *locus of control* is further exemplified in the resulting agreement lodged with the business that is signed by all parties.

In terms of locus of control, mediation is perhaps atypical of most workplace and management processes and cultures and is certainly very different from most current institutional or ad hoc responses to the breakdown of relationships in the workplace.

Mediation is 'solution/agreement' focused

The approach of mediation runs contrary to our natural and instinctual 'fight–flight' responses to conflict and is different from many standard reactions within organizations in the handling of workplace disputes. Mediation does not focus upon positions, history or blame. It puts the emphasis not on the problem but on the _solution_ and, in addition, upon the _agreement_ that will ensure that this solution is realized and maintained.

We shall examine in Chapter 3 how the instinctual dynamics of conflict result most typically in someone winning and someone consequently losing in the interaction; this can be shorthanded as a 'win–lose' outcome for the parties involved. Sometimes, when conflict is extreme, little more can be expected than a complete 'lose–lose' for all the parties involved – and this, of course, may include the organization itself as well as those involved in the initial conflict.

The structured process of mediation is, by contrast, focused upon the ground where solutions _can_ be found: namely a creative future that all parties can envisage, offering new and attractive benefits deriving from agreed changes to their working relationship. This kind of creative outcome provides the win–win solution for all concerned. Moreover the agreement that enshrines this solution can only emerge if all participants are convinced that the new outcome will better meet their particular needs, recognize their interests or deliver some significant new gain in the context of their working relationship.

In this way, mediation is about 'what people want' rather than 'what they don't want'.

In mediation the disputants offer the solution themselves

Mediation remains, therefore, a unique method of conflict resolution in that it is the participants themselves, and not any outside agency or advisor, who create and agree the solutions and strategies to resolve their issues and problems.

The structure and process of mediation enable the participants to take responsibility for generating a range of new solutions uniquely geared towards their particular needs and work interests. The process of mediation also ensures that it is the participants themselves who are ultimately accountable for the mutual acceptability, workability and success of their agreed solution. _It is both 'their problem' and 'their solution'._

This 'accountability' of the participants is also made evident in their signatures to the final agreement produced at the close of the mediation. Their accountability is thereby made public to the business in the form of the mediation voluntary agreement document that is usually lodged, at the close of the mediation, with HR or whoever instigated the mediation.

This agreement acts both as a measure of the participants' responsibility for change and as a testimony to their intention to restore their performance back into functional, respectful working relations with each other, with colleagues or team members, and essentially with the organization to whom they are contracted.

The mediator is impartial

We have already touched upon the fact that 'impartiality' is a keystone within mediation. Without impartiality mediation is simply a non-starter.

As we shall explore in more detail later, people in fight mode are mentally, emotionally and hormonally geared to instinctually overcome whatever it is that threatens them, or alternatively to retreat into the defensive. Employees in such conflicts are naturally programmed to be very sensitive to any danger to their interests and to whom exactly it is that they can see as friend, foe or even as the scapegoat in the situation. It is only through transparent impartiality that the mediator can remain credible, independent and unallied, and thereby win the right to facilitate exchanges and ultimately to help build bridges of understanding between them. The ability and skill of the experienced mediator to remain impartial is particularly important when mediating in situations of hierarchical power imbalances or in mediating complaints where discrimination (race, gender, disability etc) may be an issue or an aspect of the situation.

To be successful the mediator must display impartiality from first contact and must demonstrate it in terms of overt 'fairness and mutuality' throughout the whole process of the mediation. This is achieved in a number of ways: through the equal inclusion of all participants in the process, by the validation of experiences and feelings expressed by each of those in conflict and, finally and importantly, through the mutuality of language used by the mediator – such as the use of the word 'both' in reference to the participants – which demonstrates an equal emphasis on the meeting of everyone's needs. By the even-handed inclusion of their views and experiences, the skilful mediator can begin to build the mutual 'shared ground' that progressively opens up the prospect of lasting 'shared gain'.

One could almost liken the mediator to a juggler holding all the balls in the air at the same time, giving equal care and attention to the needs and issues of all concerned and not losing sight of any. The mediator is also skilled at holding what may appear as opposite and opposing polarities with a calm equanimity and without any need or pull to take sides.

The mediator accomplishes this in the early stages by determining the needs of all participants in the mediation and later by establishing what solutions will meet these needs. The mediator targets this directly with inclusive invitations and 'mutuality of language' such as: 'Let's see what will work for you both...' or 'Let's see what will work for all of you in this team...'

Only this impartial approach can uncover the mutual territory that can provide the guarantee of shared benefit and solutions that will last.

Mediation is confidential

As the process of mediation invites honesty and involves the sharing of views, of feelings, of needs and of future hopes, it is essential that the process is facilitated and protected by confidentiality. With regard to the organization commissioning the mediation, this means that HR and managers must not expect any reporting of the proceedings or any disclosure about the 'content' of the discussions that take place within the mediation.

What the company *will* receive, as part of the procedure, is a copy of the signed mediation agreement that forms the public outcome and marks the accountability of the participants in relation to the improvement of their working relationship. It is often the human resource department that holds this voluntary agreement in confidence for the purpose of any follow-up meetings with the parties to the mediation that may be required. Finally all parties to the mediation agree not discuss the content of the mediation outside the event.

Confidentiality also means that no other use of the mediation or of its contents may be made in any possible subsequent formal or legal procedure – nor may it be used as evidence or recorded in an individual's performance evaluation record. All that will be usually disclosed is that a mediation took place and it was successful or it was not successful.

If mediation is unsuccessful

If the mediation takes place but is unsuccessful, then further formal or legal procedures can be invoked if the parties or the organization so choose. The corollary to this is that if any formal or legal procedures or appeals are already in progress, then these actions need to be suspended or fully completed before the mediation can take place.

Mediations are usually successful (most mediation practitioners estimate an 85 per cent success rate) and this can be attributed to the clarity and boundaries of the mediation process itself, the experience and skill of the mediator and, last but not least, to the actual structure of the mediation, which ensures that it is, of its nature, constructive, positive and solution focused. It is also true that if the mediator finds, prior to the mediation or during the individual meetings with the parties, that positions are too entrenched or there is not a real willingness to resolve, then the mediator may decide not go ahead with the mediation.

Any organization or business will have a range of options and means of dealing with employee complaints and difficulties, and mediation is but one of these. If it is not appropriate or if the parties are not willing to engage in mediation, then other 'organizational means' will need to be employed.

The reason for considering mediation is simply and generically that breakdowns in interpersonal working relations are damaging to staff morale and can directly and negatively affect performance across the business or organization. The distinct advantage of mediation, as the conflict resolution method of choice, is that by helping to rebuild functional working relations, mediation restores emotional well-being, and allows people to refocus on what they are being paid to do – their job and their quality of service.

WHERE DOES WORKPLACE MEDIATION COME FROM?

Having looked at a working definition of workplace mediation and outlined some of the underlying principles, we shall end this chapter by looking briefly at the history and evolution of mediation in our times.

The origins of mediation

Mediation has been around for centuries in one form or another and appears to have been used by different societies and civilizations, including the Romans. Tribal communities around the world and American Indians also practised a form of open group or elder-led group mediation in order to resolve tribal or community issues. Some cultures regarded the mediator as a sacred figure, a shaman, a medicine man or woman who stood in between and mediated between people or between people and the spirit world.

So mediation as we know it today has gone through many permutations and transmutations and, in its modern form, has been particularly developed in the New World, in the United States and in Australia and New Zealand.

Mainstream developments

In the 1960s and the 1970s, mediation in the United States seems to have taken two divergent routes. One was the legal system, which labelled it 'alternate dispute resolution' or ADR, and the other was the adoption of mediation by grassroots community development groups, including the women's movement throughout the 1960s.

The emergence of ADR as a concept came from the growing recognition of the cost of conflict to business and industry. In business, comprehensive analyses were made of both the 'direct' and 'indirect' costs of conflict to company profitability. Direct costs included: downtime, lost production, missed deadlines and opportunities, sickness/absence, healthcare, security, compensation and legal bills. Indirect costs included: quality and productivity decline, damage to motivation and morale, effects on teamwork, customer complaints, accidents, delays and time-consuming disciplinary actions or investigations.

Clearly when company accountants began to look at the bottom line of conflict and the comparative costs of litigation and ADR, then the calculations came down firmly in favour of the early resolution, the relatively low cost and the high success rate of workplace mediation.

Ongoing academic research on the effects and effectiveness of mediation also helped confirm the trend. Kressel and Pruit (1989, with Carnevale 1992, and contributor in 2000 to Deutsch and Coleman's _Handbook of Conflict Resolution_, Chapter 25) emphasized that mediation scored well in terms of high client satisfaction – in the range of 70–90 per cent – even in cases that failed to reach agreements. This compared well with the lower satisfaction given to settlements with attorneys (66 per cent) and by the courts (40–50 per cent). Even in intractable cases, which could not be solved by attorneys, mediation resulted in settlements in 40–70 per cent of the samples. In small claims disputes, compliance with mediated agreements was rated as high as 81 per cent of the cases compared with 48 per cent for those using traditional adjudication. Finally research confirmed that mediated results were more even-handed, speedier and less costly to participants or the courts that used them.

The second mainstream trend in the development of mediation in the 1960s and 1970s was around the community-based use of mediation. The religious Society of Friends (Quakers) developed one of the longest-running mediation training programmes called the Friends Conflict Resolution Program of the Philadelphia Yearly Meeting. To this day, mediation remains a natural and important part of the Quaker Peace Movement around the world. Now mediation can be found in an ever increasing number of sectors – community, family, divorce, medical, in schools, environmental, in restorative justice and in international politics – and, of course, in the workplace.

Theoretical roots and developments in practice

In its early forms, within labour relations, mediation was essentially a mode of 'problem solving' and the emphasis was mainly on the nature, fairness, equality and viability of the resulting outcome agreements. New theoretical impetus arrived in the 1950s and 1960s with the development of social psychology by Kurt Lewin at MIT and the T-group dynamics pioneered at Bethel by the National Training Laboratories.

Nonviolent communication (NVC), as developed widely by Marshall B Rosenberg, began during the 1960s in the United States and has provided a solid base for the specific communication skills for both peacekeeping and mediation. NVC is founded on language and communication skills that strengthen our ability to remain compassionate and human.

Further developments in thinking such as Deutsch's work on conflict (1973) and the Harvard Negotiation Project (Fisher and Ury, 1981) helped both to expand the understanding of conflict and to evolve the process of 'deal making' into a more refined process of 'interest-based sharing' with a view to 'generating options for mutual gain – based on objective criteria'. In *The Resolution of Conflict: Constructive and Destructive Processes* (1973) Morton Deutsch differentiated between destructive and constructive conflict – the constructive possibility being where: 'parties believe that all sides can attain important goals and results in solutions satisfactory to all that produce a general feeling that the parties have gained something.'

Within the practice of mediation the initial focus upon problem solving and agreements was expanded further by the work of Bush and Folger in *The Promise of Mediation: Responding to Conflict through Empowerment and Recognition* (1994). Their approach and accompanying style of mediation was termed 'transformational' and claimed that: 'The benefit of conflict transformation – that is changing the quality of the conflict interaction – is more valuable than the other benefits that mediation can be used to produce'.

Our position, as authors, is that the 'six-step model' of mediation and our particular approach look to preserve the goals both of 'transformation' and of 'solution finding' within the workplace mediation process. We acknowledge the power and the transformative and potentially healing nature of the mediation process upon those involved; while at the same time looking to facilitate targeted and specific behavioural agreements for improvements that will express, preserve and ensure the lasting transformation of the ground of conflict.

Organized mediation and professional training

Conflict resolution as a subject comes under the auspices of many academic institutions and departments, but it is over the past 10 years that the specialist arena of mediation for workplace disputes emerged. When the authors first began their work in the UK, there was little or no workplace mediation sector, even though community and family mediation were quite well established. It was in 1998 that PMR Ltd designed and created the first nationally accredited professional training in workplace mediation in the UK, leading the way for several similar courses to be created thereafter.

Alongside a whole range of highly experienced and dedicated individual entrepreneurs, from the fields of management consultancy, human resources, NLP, psychotherapy, education and training, independent mediation consultants like PMR Ltd and its associates played a significant part in bringing mediation into UK organizations from the mid-1990s to the present time, developing both theory and practice simultaneously. ACAS (the Advisory, Conciliation and Arbitration Service), a UK statutory body, and other UK management institutions and colleges appear to have entered the field of workplace mediation later on, in around 2005 and onwards.

The contemporary scene and the stance of the UK government

It is clear in recent years in the UK that workplace mediation has received much attention as a method for the resolution of workplace conflict and as a preferred alternative to the mounting backlog of tribunals and litigation.

Experiences and complaints of bullying in the workplace are on the increase, and unfortunately the means and ways of bullying such as 'cyber bullying' through web pages, e-mails and texts are also on the rise. A recent UK survey of 4,000 employees (The Fair Treatment at Work Survey, DTI, 2007) found that almost a million employees said they had personally experienced bullying or harassment, and that women and employees with disabilities were more likely to have been bullied.

Organizations have moved from the perception that 'it does not happen here' to more acceptance that bullying does happen and to the introduction of policies to try to address the problem. Adopting a zero tolerance of bullying and harassment means adopting a whole range or continuum of dispute resolution methods to tackle it, from informal methods to formal disciplinary investigations or dismissal. Mediation is one of these informal dispute methods and is best suited for less serious complaints, complaints that involve difficult personal feelings and issues on both sides or where it is one person's word against another's.

If offered at an early stage, a mediation can positively help people understand the impact of their behaviour or language and instigate changes in that behaviour. According to the Chartered Institute of Personnel and Development (CIPD, 2007), organizations that provide mediation training to staff receive fewer tribunal claims than those that do not.

Business and industry continue to evaluate the burdensome cost of conflict: according to the CIPD a third of employers now believe that disputes are less likely to be resolved now than they were before statutory procedures were put in place. In addition tribunals are said to typically take up 350 days of management time per year in the UK and employers spend an average of £20,000 a year on tribunals. And this does not even include the cost and the indirect disruption of experienced people leaving a company because of ongoing conflict. Recruiting and re-training new staff can very expensive and the cost of recruitment alone is calculated to be at least one-third of a person's annual salary.

Government for its part is clearly concerned about the cost of conflict and the over-reliance on legal forms of redress. In December of 2006 the Secretary of State for Trade and Industry launched a root and branch review of government support for resolving disputes in the workplace saying –

> By reducing the numbers of disputes, and resolving those that do happen more quickly, we can raise the UK's productivity and ensure better employer relations. We can also cut the cost of dealing with disputes, which can be substantial. At the same time, we are determined to protect the rights of employees and ensure that they have access to justice.

> (Press release, 7 December 2006)

The result of this initiative – the Gibbons Report on *Better Dispute Resolution*, released in March 2007 – points out the extent of the problem that conflict poses at work, quoting research that claims that around 1.7 million people (6.9 per cent of employees) said that they had been unfairly treated at work on the grounds of their personal characteristics (eg, sex, race, age or appearance).

The report in its recommendations laments the current 'one size fits all' use of formal resolution procedures, and endorses the use of mediation as a preferred strategy whilst avoiding making it mandatory. The report also advocates the streamlining of tribunals to reduce bureaucracy and *early informal resolution through mediation* following the successful examples of employment conflict reduction in the United States and New Zealand.

Of mediation itself the Gibbons Report says:

> Mediation and other alternative dispute resolution techniques are effective means of achieving early resolution. However in the current system parties tend to get caught up in process rather than focusing on achieving an early acceptable outcome... It is clear that the earlier a dispute is settled, the better it will normally be for all concerned e.g. in terms of disruption to business and lives, and associated costs. Early resolution can also involve outcomes not available through the tribunal system such as a positive job reference, an apology, explanation and changes in behaviour.

Having introduced the nature, principles, history and development of workplace mediation we shall examine workplace conflict in the next chapter with an example of a typical breakdown in a working relationship.

Chapter 1: The essentials

This chapter is about the definition and the working principles of mediation. A definition of workplace mediation is:

> Mediation is a structured process whereby an impartial mediator facilitates communication between those in dispute in order for them to understand each other better and for them to come up with mutually acceptable solutions that will improve the working relationship in the future.

Mediation is all about focusing people on what they want, rather than what they don't want.

Mediation, as a dispute resolution method, is quite specific and is based on several operational principles: it is voluntary, solution-focused, and confidential; the mediator is impartial; the parties to the mediation come up with their own voluntary agreements; and if mediation is unsuccessful, formal or legal procedures can be invoked.

Mediation has emerged over this century first in the context of labour relations and then by extension as a prime tool of ADR (alternative dispute resolution). The thinking and practice of mediation have evolved together with our understanding of conflict to include the 'transformational' as well as the 'problem-solving' and solutions aspects of conflict resolution.

The practice of mediation has grown and professional training and development for workplace mediators is now widely available.

In the contemporary view of government in the UK, mediation is one of the preferred forms of intervention in workplace conflict that can produce significant early agreement in ways that avoid the damage, delays, costs and the bureaucracy of the current 'one size fits all' recourse to formal legal tribunals.

2
An example of a breakdown in a workplace relationship:
Wendy and Mark

In this chapter we shall describe a typical example of the breakdown of workplace relationships in everyday business life and examine more closely what it is likely to entail. As with all the examples used in this book, the story of Wendy and Mark is fictional but is based upon, or is sometimes a composite of, experiences drawn from real life.

WENDY AND MARK AND A COMPLAINT OF BULLYING

Wendy has worked with her line manager Mark for nearly five years. Initially they got on well – in fact at one time there was a bit of talk around the office about how well they got on. Over the last 18 months, however, their previously productive and friendly relationship has deteriorated into a morass of ill-defined allegations and counter-allegations about each other's conduct at work.

In essence, Wendy now states that during the company reorganization that has been taking place over the previous year, she has been subjected to active discrimination at the hands of Mark. Wendy claims that she has been insulted in public, that her competence and productivity have been repeatedly called into question and that she has now been overlooked for a natural promotion in the new structure. Wendy blames Mark's overt and covert discrimination for this unjust and untenable situation.

For his part, Mark claims that Wendy has taken an inexplicable dislike to him over the last 18 months. He asserts that all her complaints and negative attitude are completely without substance. However, Mark claims that the overall effect of Wendy's progressive change of attitude has indeed been to decrease her effectiveness and productivity at work. Mark claims that this explains why he did not promote Wendy when she would have been the natural choice for the post.

Over the last six months the situation has escalated. Mark first aired his concerns with his own line manager and said that he was contemplating initial disciplinary action in conjunction with a 'competency assessment' linked to an ongoing monitoring of Wendy's performance. Wendy, during the same period, approached both the company human resource department and her trade union representative to indicate that she now wished to raise a formal grievance against Mark for repeated adverse actions and decisions that she is now claiming amount to a process of constructive dismissal.

The latest development is that Wendy has been absent from work for over two weeks and has just returned a doctor's note to indicate that she is suffering from multiple stress-related symptoms and is being offered medication and a recovery absence from work that could be up to three months' duration.

Does this sound familiar? The situation is based upon fact – the names and details have been changed to protect the innocent.

The most interesting thing in the above scenario, however, is not so much the particular complexities of the situation as the fact that Mark and Wendy are not unusual people. They are no more abnormal or disturbed than are most of us and both have actually been acknowledged achievers in the organization over previous years.

SO HOW DO ORGANIZATIONS RESPOND TO CONFLICT?

We can all make guesses as to what might have happened in the working relationship between Wendy and Mark. Our guesses might be right or they might be wrong. Such investigatory guessing and assumption making is interestingly often the first recourse of those called in to help in such situations.

Often managers or HR who are involved will devote their attention to 'why' the relationship breakdown has occurred, and will first look for the details and as many facts as they can find. This understandable question can however lead to complications. In essence, the search for the 'why?' will actually highlight the points of conflict in the various stories. This in turn becomes the ground upon which organizational members then come to 'takes sides', to make judgements or ascribe blame.

In the end, whether the guesses as to the 'why?' are right or whether they are wrong, they will make little difference to the outcome in the workplace. In fact, these judgements may actually complicate things – sometimes beyond repair.

In essence, what will matter in the longer term is not 'why' the breakdown has occurred but rather what range of workplace solutions are open to Wendy and Mark or to their managers, HR or any other internal support agents. In a nutshell, the ultimate question that governs the success or failure of any managerial or organizational intervention is: 'What prospect does it offer for a successful resolution that will restore performance for the company that employs Wendy and Mark and, at the same time, achieve a satisfactory resolution for both Mark and Wendy?'

If you have ever been involved in, or witnessed, a Wendy and Mark breakdown of working relationships, then you will probably know how little there usually is out there that can be called upon to effectively resolve the situation either before or after it has escalated to the complex interpersonal scenario so far described.

You may have witnessed in such situations the use of internal business processes and procedures such as complaints, grievances, third-party investigations, disciplinary hearings or other HR and manager-led interventions. Inevitably the drawback of such interventions, as we shall shortly see, is that of their nature they are highly adversarial, *blame-based* and tend to generate '*winners and losers*' – as those involved feel it necessary to build their case against each other. These usual interventions do little to encourage any kind of mutual understanding and can steer people like Wendy and Mark into a long-drawn-out, highly stressful formal action.

In the worst scenario, such interventions can mean that more and more complaints end up in employment tribunals or – given our rapidly growing culture of compensation – more cases will result in civil litigation.

Our contention in this book is that there is a different and rapidly growing solution designed to address the breakdown of such complex workplace relationships: namely workplace mediation. This is a unique and discreet process that offers a radically different approach to the dilemma of a relationship breakdown. It does so within a process that respects all parties and that excludes any form of discrimination or partiality towards each and every participant. The clear and unique purpose of mediation is to seek a solution that is participant-generated, mutually agreed and within which nobody is a 'loser'.

Chapter 2: The essentials

This chapter tells the story of a typical workplace conflict – in this case, between Wendy and Mark. Wendy feels discriminated against and badly treated by Mark, her manager, who in turn feels frustrated by what he sees as Wendy's negative attitude and decreased productivity. The situation escalates to allegations and counter-allegations.

'Investigatory guessing' or use of grievances and other policies can lead to unhelpful judgements and ascribing blame and do little to help Wendy and Mark understand each other or find options for resolution.

Mediation is a radically different approach to the dilemmas and complexities of the breakdown of interpersonal relationships at work and is a 'unique and discreet process', which encourages understanding and options for ways forward.

3

Just how does mediation work?

Having examined the definition and principles underlying workplace mediation and outlined a typical breakdown in a working relationship between the characters of Wendy and Mark, we shall set out, in this chapter, to put flesh on the bones of the mediation process and to describe in detail the six-step structure that governs the delivery of mediation as proposed in this book.

Just to say a little about how we came to this particular mediation model. Nora Doherty studied the many mediation models (with similar stages but a different number of steps) that can be found in different countries around the world, and in 1996 she decided to create her own model out of these many and to synthesize them into a clearer six-step format. This six-step model has not only proved highly successful in practice, it is now leading the way in the organizational and business mediation sector and appears to have been adopted by many others in the mediation field. PMR has pioneered the clarity and use of this six-step model within a whole range of organizations and within the workplace in particular.

You will see in Figure 3.1 the overall sequence of a mediation and we will look more closely in the following section at the six-step model of a joint mediation meeting.

Arranging a mediation

- Initial complaint or request for a mediation.
- Manager, HR person or mediation coordinator speaks to both parties to get their agreement to mediate.
- Mediator is selected – internally or externally.
- Parties receive 'mediation information' so they understand what to expect.
- A date for the mediation is agreed.

The mediation

- The mediator enters the scene.
- The mediator has individual meetings with each party.
- They are then brought together into a joint six-step structured mediation meeting/s with the mediator, which ends with the signing of the mediation voluntary agreements.
- A follow-up meeting with the mediator and the parties in the mediation takes place at some agreed time in the future in order to see how the agreements are working out; this marks the end of the mediator's role.

After the mediation

- It is up to the parties themselves to abide by the voluntary agreements they signed up to.
- If any further problems arise, they can either request another facilitated mediation meeting or other organisational means are employed to deal with the situation.

Figure 3.1 The overall sequence of a mediation

THE SIX-STEP MODEL OF MEDIATION

The structure of a workplace mediation face-to-face meeting can be synthesized into six distinct steps. One could sub-categorize these into fewer or more steps, but this overall six-step model gives a functional direction and structure to a mediation and is particularly suited to workplace mediation and repairing or restoring working relations. Each of these six steps is essential to a successful mediation and there is an important logic and psychology operating in the ordering of each of these steps.

This does not imply, however, that mediation is only a linear process nor that steps will not intermingle or be anticipated or reprised along the way. Like all models it is helpful but, in reality, one must be flexible and follow the flow of the people with whom you are mediating. The six-step model does however provide a sound guide to the process and structure of all the necessary parts and stages of mediation.

The process begins with the mediator/s having private, confidential individual meetings with each of the parties involved, and then moves to bringing the participants together in a joint face-to-face structured mediation meeting.

The six steps of the face-to-face mediation comprise:
1. Introduction and ground rules.
2. Hearing what has happened and summarizing back.
3. Identifying and discussing the issues.
4. Mutual understanding and communicating feelings.
5. Idea-storming and exploring win–win solutions.
6. Signing the voluntary agreements and arranging a follow-up meeting.

Before examining each of these steps in more detail, we will first look at the purpose and conduct of the 'individual mediation meetings' (see Figure 3.2).

Individual meetings with the mediator

It is important to the success of the mediation that each participant entering the process is 'listened to well'. This is done in the individual meetings held with each person involved in the mediation. This initial meeting may last an hour or two and serves a number of important purposes.

In the first place, it is likely that the mediator will not have met the participants in person prior to the event, and so the first obvious purpose of the individual meeting is as a rapport-building and 'getting to know you' event, and a chance to hear from each person what they feel has been happening. It may also be that this is the first time that those in conflict have been given complete attention and have been fully listened to by someone who has no agenda of their own.

The process of mediation relies on effective communication delivered in the context of an enabling relationship. The individual meeting provides both an important first exchange and the chance for the participants themselves to assess the safety of the relationship being offered by the mediator.

We have seen that people coming to mediation may be feeling considerable tension, hurts or fears arising both from the conflict itself and possibly from uncertainty about the experience that they are about to

> ### THE SIX-STEP STRUCTURE OF A FACE-TO-FACE MEDIATION MEETING

After the mediator has had individual meetings with each of the parties involved

1. INTRODUCTIONS AND AGREEING GROUND RULES

- Mediator sets the positive purpose of the mediation
- Agreeing the mediation ground rules:
  - no interrupting when the other is speaking
  - treating each other in a respectful manner
  - confidentiality of discussions

2. HEARING WHAT HAS HAPPENED AND SUMMARIZING

- Mediator asks each person 'What do you feel has been happening in your working relationship?'
- Mediator listens and summarizes back for each person

3. IDENTIFYING AND DISCUSSING THE ISSUES

- Clarifying and prioritizing the underlying issues (mediator may put these on a flipchart)
- Discussion of each of the main issues

4. MUTUAL UNDERSTANDING AND COMMUNICATING FEELINGS

- Encouraging mutual understanding and direct communication with each other: 'Perhaps you would like to say directly to... what you found unacceptable'

5. IDEA-STORMING AND WIN–WIN SOLUTIONS

- 'What needs to happen for things to improve between you?'
- Exploring a range of possible win–win solutions
- Parties agree on the mutual agreements, including the specific details

6. SIGNING THE VOLUNTARY AGREEMENTS

- Mediator writes up the voluntary agreements and each person signs it (in certain cases, agreements may be 'verbal only' if agreed beforehand)
- A 'follow-up' meeting with the mediator is agreed at a future date to see how the agreements are working out

© PMR Ltd 1996

Figure 3.2 The six-step structure of face-to-face joint mediation

Purpose of the individual meetings with the mediator

The goals are to:

▪ hear directly what has been happening from the participant's perspective;

▪ listen, give good attention and build rapport and trust;

▪ assess and discuss whether mediation is appropriate and agree on the boundaries and conditions of the mediation;

▪ assess the best means of setting up the mediation joint meeting;

▪ enable the individual to explore and clarify issues and concerns;

▪ answer questions about the mediation joint face-to-face meeting – ground rules, confidentiality etc;

▪ give parties the chance to 'express feelings' and say in confidence what they want to say – whilst, at the same time, maintaining mediator impartiality and confidentiality;

▪ encourage parties to be clear that they do, in fact, wish to find a resolution through the mediation process;

▪ set the positive purpose of the mediation and what they can expect to gain from it.

undertake. The participants will of course already have had some information about the nature and purpose of the mediation. They may also have checked out any queries or reservations prior to agreeing to engage in the event. Nevertheless arriving at the actual mediation event can be daunting and can re-stimulate hurts or anger and perhaps revive threatening issues. This in turn may provoke the need to self-justify or to express feelings and fears about other people involved in the event.

By talking with each participant individually the mediator is able to do a number of important things. Firstly, these meetings offer participants the space to simply 'tell their story' and, in the course of doing so, to vent their feelings. This is as much for the sake of the participant as the mediator and is quite different in nature from the detailed information gathering and questioning that accompanies a formal investigation process.

Mediators, by their approach to these initial meetings, actively demonstrate that they are not engaging in any prior analysis or judgements of the situation and are not concerned with apportioning blame or with the vindication of anybody's particular position. What the mediator *is* offering is impartial listening and an acceptance of the issues and feelings, simply as expressed by each participant. Added to this the mediator will also hear and acknowledge what someone is saying but without entering into any agreement with what he or she has heard and without colluding with anyone. In this initial meeting the mediator will also review and check the positive intention of the participants and to assure their willingness to change things for the better. In addition, the mediator will be able to demonstrate open, positive attitudes and even anticipate the potential important gains that may be achieved by everyone from the coming event.

By the end of this first meeting then, the participants should be able to feel that they have been received impartially and acceptingly, that the mediator has accurately understood the significance of their issues and feelings, and that the mediator is neither taking sides nor prescribing in any way what anyone should do to resolve the problem.

In order to ensure the safety of the event, the mediator will also use the opportunity to go over what mediation is, what they can expect at the joint mediation meeting and what the ground rules entail.

Finally, the initial meeting provides the mediator with a last check that mediation is actually appropriate to the situation. It may also give clues about how best to set up the mediation, such as whether anyone else needs to be part of the mediation face-to-face meeting, or be an opportunity to make sure that all formal or legal processes have been suspended or fully completed.

Having covered the role and significance of the individual meetings, we move next to examine the actual six-step sequence of mediation viewed from the perspective of both the mediator and participants.

Step 1: Introductions and ground rules

The mediator sets the overall direction of the mediation and the structure of mediation and, in this sense, mediation is not client-led. Mediation is unlike comparable models of personal counselling or self-directed problem solving. It is the mediator who is responsible for the overall management or direction of the six-step model, but it is the parties themselves that lead the *content and the solutions* within the mediation. As such, the mediation process ensures that it is *their problem* that is described and owned and it is *their agreements* that are achieved.

The process and the overall structure of the event belongs therefore with the mediator, but the will and the responsibility for finding a way forward, towards a positive mutual agreement, remains with the parties themselves.

In this first of the six steps of mediation, the control and structuring of the process falls very definitely to the initiative of the mediator. Usually this first step of mediation will include a number of elements:

▌ briefly setting out clear boundaries for the event, checking understandings and expectations and allaying any remaining worries so as to clear the ground for a helpful beginning;

▌ stating the positive purpose of the mediation and obtaining a final commitment as to the willingness of the participants to work towards agreements for the improvement of their workplace relationship;

▌ a re-statement of, and an agreement to, the 'ground rules' of mediation.

The ground rules of mediation that the authors use are:

1. That while one person is speaking, the other does not interrupt – as they will both get equal time to say what they wish to say.
2. That they treat each other in a respectful manner.
3. That the content of the discussions during the mediation are 'confidential'.

The ground rules are important in mediation as they establish the basis of 'respectful' communication. Agreement to the ground rules allows the mediator to manage the communication so that it remains as constructive as possible throughout the whole of the mediation. The danger is that without ground rules being agreed at the beginning, the mediation meeting could well deteriorate into destructive emotional reactions and put-downs.

Step 2: Hearing what has happened and summarizing back for each person

In the first step of mediation, the mediator asks the participants to briefly say what they feel has been happening in their working relationship and then summarizes back for each one. In this way, each party hears, possibly for the first time, how the other person is viewing the situation.

What the mediator invites in this opening exchange is not a recounting of *anything and everything* that has occurred between the participants, still less a *history starting from day one* of their dispute. An invitation along such lines would elicit a catalogue of complaints and a morass of historical detail.

By asking the question 'Can you tell me, what has been happening in your working relationship?' the mediator steers the event from the outset towards the single focus that will produce the necessary change – namely the reconstruction of the working relationship. The mediator then reframes and summarizes back what he or she has heard. This more neutral recap of a person's perception of what has been going on lays the foundation for the more constructive form of communication through the rest of the mediation meeting.

Step 3: Identifying and discussing the issues

Having asked for brief outlines from both parties as to 'what has happened' and having understood the effect that the conflict has had upon the working relationship of the participants, the mediator is then in a position to address the next step: the identification of issues.

At this point the discussions are widened to elicit the real and underlying issues that are between those in conflict. Through these discussions and the use of clarifying questions and of summarizing, the mediator will be able to uncover and to check with both parties what the issues are; these may be written up on a flipchart by the mediator if more than one or two issues are identified.

This clarification of the underlying issues can be described as something like finding the golden nuggets within the complex and emotionally laden stories that each party recounts. Getting to the real issues leads directly to possible agreements: '*get to the real issues and the agreements will follow.*'

It will be helpful here to touch upon a psychological model that aligns the participant's 'positions', 'issues' and 'needs' with the desired outcome. These are illustrated in Figure 3.3 below. If the two triangles represent the awareness of the two participants, then the apex represents the usual starting place in conflicts that is characterized by division and distance. At this point people are concerned to defend their *position* against the opposing party. In this restrictive sector of conflict there can be no exchange that does not somehow accentuate differences and reinforce negative stances and positions.

If however the mediator is able to translate statements of *position* into underlying *issues*, *values* and *interests* and ultimately to uncover the *needs* of the participants, then solutions based upon shared ground are possible. At this wider level of shared issues and needs, new territory opens up in which participants can begin to hear, and come first to accept each other's values, and second to satisfy their disclosed needs.

It is on the basis of increasing the awareness of their 'shared ground' that agreements offering shared gain become a possibility. The mediator therefore employs this psychology in Step 3 of the mediation model by playing down any re-statement of positions. The greater the focus on

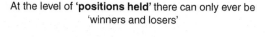

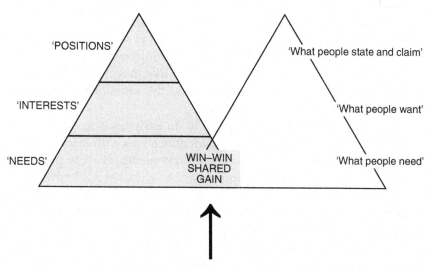

At the level of **'positions held'** there can only ever be 'winners and losers'

'POSITIONS'

'INTERESTS'

'NEEDS'

WIN–WIN
SHARED
GAIN

'What people state and claim'

'What people want'

'What people need'

From within the overlap territory
and shared ground of 'interests' and 'needs'
participants can generate win–win agreements

Figure 3.3 'Positions', 'interests' and 'needs'

difference, the greater will be the concern as to *who wins and who loses*. The mediator will be looking instead to promote a deeper recognition of the real issues involved and to affirm the individual values and needs that these issues represent.

It is at this deeper level of exchange that both the shared ground and the possibility of a win–win situation can emerge.

Step 4: Mutual understanding and communicating feelings

It may appear odd that the communication of feelings is separated out as a step and is placed chronologically after the examination of positions, issues and needs. This is, however, sound psychology.

As we all know much of the dynamic of conflict involves strong feelings. The 'fight–flight' syndrome mobilizes high adrenalin levels that provide us with the necessary emergency energy to resist and to overcome danger. This drive includes the raw motivating emotions of anger, fear, anxiety or even (when faced with insurmountable obstacles from which the person must self-protect) feelings of hopelessness or depression. Although these feelings are natural they tend, early on in the mediation, to complicate rather than to assist conflict resolution.

This is not to say that feelings can be ignored or should be suppressed. In fact, unlike other forms of dispute resolution, mediation does allow and gives space to such feelings. It is simply that in Steps 1 to 3, the mediator will not be actively seeking to expand this emotional ground or to encourage the expressions of such feeling.

What the mediator will be looking to do early on is to acknowledge emotions as they emerge but to avoid identifications with emotions as the source of the problems. Early positional statements, like 'the problem is that he is being completely unreasonable' or ' she does not know how to manage people at all', would not benefit from being expanded or explored as they might be, say, in the context of personal counselling. Such exploration and the consequent enlargement of these feeling-based identifications could open the door to a spiral of projections, of introspection or a series of interpretative exchanges of 'amateur psychology' or misconstrued assumptions about the other. So in the earlier stages of the mediation process, the mediator will seek simply to acknowledge such feeling statements or emotional identifications without any judgements or the need to take sides.

When we explore the psychology of conflict in more detail in Chapter 12, we shall draw upon the interpersonal psychology of 'Transactional Analysis' and characterize this uninformed emotionality as the 'child'. Employing this model we shall see that lasting agreements to resolve conflict are more likely to result from the 'adult' state that is characterized by rationality, objectivity and a willingness to understand the other.

So if feelings are not expected to 'drive' the mediation process, what then are their place and their value in Step 4 of the mediation process? In point of fact, feelings can play a powerful role in this later stage of mediation both in deepening the process and in ensuring the lasting success of the agreement.

Unlike most other forms of dispute resolution, mediation does invite and allow the safe expression of feelings. The value and role of feelings then can be threefold, as outlined in the box below.

The role of feelings in mediation

▌ In the later stages of mediation 'disclosure of feeling' can dramatically deepen 'shared ground' and sometimes supply testimony to the common experience of being fully human. It helps people understand the other or understand the impact that their behaviour has had upon them.

▌ The linking of emotions to future solutions can also powerfully inform and support the participants in working out just what it could be like to enjoy a brighter and happier working future.

▌ Finally, the whole mediation experience can be cemented by sharing typically difficult emotions that participants have to deal with during this unique experience. Sometimes this bonding effect can mark a watershed in their relationship and often a turning point in the mediation itself.

The reason that feeling is located in this later step in the mediation process is that it plays a powerful supporting role in deepening what emerges as personally significant to the participants. Of course, the mediator cannot demand this level of personal disclosure, but s/he can invite it or give it space when it feels right to do so.

> Until people really feel heard and understood – in terms of their feelings – then they will not be ready or prepared to move on and look at solutions.
>
> Nora Doherty

As such these more open and honest exchanges can unite and even heal in a way that is quite different from the rational work of producing an agreement.

Step 5: Idea-storming and exploring 'win–win' solutions

Having analysed the conflicted situation by exploring the issues and needs of the participants, and having also provided the opportunity for associated emotional sharing, the mediator can now move towards the agenda of agreed solutions and of something better. In essence, this is accomplished through the power and the dynamic of futures.

At this point we need to establish that it is a neurological fact that brains are future driven. Once the brain can conceive of an outcome (one that can be seen, heard and felt in detail and that is experienced as highly desirable and motivational) then we are actually only one or more steps away from achieving it.

Up to the point of commencing the mediation, the neurologies of the participants are likely to have been firmly engaged with negatives and may have already produced damaging outcomes and generated painful emotions. This is sometimes evident if one asks the participants at their individual meeting about what they want. Their response may well be stated solely in negatives. These may include: 'to get away from so and so', or 'to prove to the business that I am right (and that the other is wrong)', 'to stop so and so behaving badly towards me', to 'have them sacked', or maybe to 'go back to things as they were before these changes' and so on. Clearly all negative focuses.

Such positions, as we have seen, are powerfully compounded by the associated emotions of hurt, anger, fear, anxiety or depression. With such negative mind-sets any subsequent workplace contacts are likely to cause further flare-ups and to re-stimulate hurts or rekindle the conflict so that their positions become reinforced. Within Step 5 of the mediation process, then, the mediator looks to reverse this negative history by initiating a positive and future-based process that will help guide and transform thinking. The heart of this dynamic is one or more versions of 'the golden question' that in essence comes down to *'How would you like things to be?'* This question can be expressed, however, in a great many conversational forms, as shown in the box below.

Forms of 'the golden question'

'What might work for you?'

'If you could get things exactly the way you would really like them to be... what would it look like?'

'If you were to wake up tomorrow and say we no longer have a problem... what would that take?'

'If you could imagine a way forward here, what might it be?'

In essence, by using such questions, the mediator is inviting the participants' combined neurologies to abandon the negative 'framing' of their present outcomes and to throw open the door instead to a range of desirable, unlimited possibilities for a new and motivating workplace relationship and hence for a better future workplace relationship. *Focus on what you want – not on what you don't want!*

At this point useful tools are the classic 'idea-storming' or open exploration of possibilities for resolution. This provides a valuable method for generating the practical 'how-to's' needed to work out the strategies, the changes or the actions that will be needed to support the new and desirable shared outcomes.

Idea-storm rules are simple. Those taking part adopt a creative stance – free from all self or mutual censorship – and generate in turn and without comment as many creative futures or 'how-to' possibilities as they can. These possibilities can be as wild or unlikely as imagination will allow but the process simply carries on in turn until both run out of ideas. They then sort and refine these possibilities with a more critical and analytical eye, looking for the solutions that generate the most excitement, the best payoff and the greatest benefits to all parties.

Whatever the methodology – from flip chart or 'post-it' idea-storming, to rational and logical discussion or perhaps a more visual 'future-based' vision – the underlying dynamic remains the same. The mediator is essentially looking for a light-up of vital signs in the morale and physiology of the participants indicating that they have come up with something significantly better. That 'something' may be a future-based picture, a specific key solution that will make all the difference, a change in how they communicate with each other, or changes in work practices to which they feel they can both commit.

Step 6: Signing the voluntary agreement and arranging a follow-up meeting

The journey from generating 'what they really want' to signing up to the agreement is an important one involving a number of tests that must be satisfied if the new outcome is to be achievable and if the participants are to leave with a document that is capable of supporting their new intentions. In essence the agreement must put in place specific 'how-to's' that will mark the transition from where they are now to their new goal and where they want to be ideally.

However this agreement is expressed – whether in broad strategic terms or in detailed action planning – it must amount to a plan that can support both a new understanding between the participants and the specific actions or improvements that will ensure that the working relationship and their workplace productivity and effectiveness is actually renewed.

This means in effect that the agreement must pass all the tests shown in the box below to guarantee that it is capable of supporting their chosen outcome and of being sustained.

In essence, the agreement must be:

■ *Specific.* It must be describable in concrete and behavioural terms not simply as vague generalities or unsupported 'good intentions'.
■ *Stated as positives rather than negatives.* It describes what people will do, rather than what they will not do or will avoid doing.
■ *Wholly in the control of the participants who must action it.* There is no point in expecting managers, the team, the business or any other outside agency to deliver what it is the participants' responsibility to bring into being and to sustain.
■ *Something that brings to each participant a visibly desirable gain or resolution.* Nobody ever put anything into something that they felt brought them only a moderate gain or even lost them ground.
■ *Actionable steps that can be immediately put into practice.* If all the actions are not immediately possible, then they should be at least planned within as short a time scale as possible and given a targeted date.
■ *Monitored results.* The participants' outcomes should preferably be supported with checks or with a feedback loop that will tell them how they are doing and what has been achieved to that point.
■ *Signed and dated.* Finally, the agreement should be signed and dated by all participants and returned as testimony of their agreement to their business.

This mediation agreement then forms, as it were, the public outcome – and also the feedback from the mediation to the business or organization. The agreement will normally be deposited with HR or with the commissioning manager as testimony of the intentions and accountability of the participants.

It should, however, be accepted by the organization that the agreement relates only to the outcome of the mediation, that it is held in confidence and will not be added to personal performance records. It cannot therefore be used as evidence in any other business complaint or grievance, process or disciplinary hearing. In any further formal process, it can simply be stated that mediation took place and that agreements were made or that the mediation was unsuccessful and no agreements were made.

Finally, these voluntary agreements will include attending a follow-up meeting with the mediator at a specific future date when the participants will meet with the mediator to review how the agreements are working out. This meeting is important as it supports parties in implementing their agreements and in sustaining the improvements in their working relationship. The meeting acts as a review and is not intended to be a further mediation and, as such, concludes the process of mediation and the involvement of the mediator.

CONFIDENTIALITY IN MEDIATION

Because confidentiality is a central principle in all sectors of mediation and contributes to both the success and the integrity of the mediation process itself, it is worth expanding on it further. The private and confidential nature of the mediation meetings is one of the reasons why employees and managers choose it over the public and recorded formal processes. Of course, if the matter is more serious and definitely a disciplinary matter, then mediation should not be considered and the situation should be fully investigated in the public domain.

Where mediation is appropriate, however, parties must trust that they can speak freely in mediation without words being taken out of context or used against them. It is this free and open expression that underpins the effectiveness of mediation communication and the kind of shifts of viewpoints that can take place as people begin to understand each other better.

It is also worth pointing out here that there may be times when a mediator needs to put some limits to this confidentiality. For example, when the authors were undertaking a team mediation within a social services residential home, we made it clear, before the mediation took place, that 'if any abuse or harm to clients or staff should emerge from our meetings, then we were legally bound to inform the authorities'. It is important that mediators know and keep in mind who they may be working for, and also be very clear with people, so they know exactly what they are contracting into when they agree to mediate.

Mediation is confidential in the following ways:

▪ The mediation is conducted in a private space (away from the everyday work space and work colleagues).

▪ The number of people who know a mediation is taking place is usually kept to the minimum (ie, the initiator of the mediation, who may be a manager or a human resource person, and the parties themselves).

▪ The 'content' of all the discussions within the mediation process is confidential.

▪ The individual meetings with the mediator (which take place before the joint face-to-face mediation meeting when the mediator brings the parties together) are also confidential. The mediator will not refer to any content from these individual meetings during the face-to-face mediation. If any of the participants wish to bring something up themselves, then that is their choice but the mediator gives them the respect and confidentiality to make this decision for themselves and will not force an issue. For instance, a person may speak very strongly about all sorts of things in the individual meetings and may choose not to refer to them again or talk in this way when they are with the other person. What parties to a mediation wish to share with each other is their choice.

▌ No recording of the mediation is retained except for the voluntary mediation agreements. This means that if any notes are taken by the mediator or any notes written up on a flipchart, these are destroyed at the end of the mediation.

▌ The written mediation agreements, which are usually the end result of the mediation (unless pre-decided to be verbal agreements only), are held by the parties themselves, the mediator (for the follow-up meeting) and whoever coordinates or instigates mediation within the organization. The agreements are not public property, are not put into any work records, and are kept confidentially by the organization. They are not used in any future complaint or legal process and if any formal request is made (ie, by an employment tribunal or court), then the only information usually released is that a mediation took place, the date and between whom, and that it was successful or it was not successful.

▌ There is no further 'public' sharing of what transpired at a mediation and there is no direct enforcement of the mediation agreements. Mediation is a fair and private way of talking about differences or difficulties. The quality of communication that is possible within this kind of privacy, facilitated by a skilled third person, is why most people who choose mediation end up with some useful agreements. It gives people the chance to hear each other out and to look at what changes of behaviour are needed to make a difference in how they work and operate together. Mediators are not enforcers or 'mediation police'. It will be up to the parties themselves to abide by their agreements. People cannot undo behaviours of the past but they can acknowledge their part in what has arisen, what the consequences were and, with this new awareness, make new choices. They need to be given the responsibility and the freedom to behave differently.

▌ If it does not work, if someone does not change his or her behaviour as agreed, then it means the organization will have to move on from mediation and look at other organizational means such as disciplinary action or whatever is appropriate to the actual future complaint that may be lodged.

MEDIATION AND LEVELS OF LISTENING

From our treatment of the mediation structure and model to this point, it is clear that the communication skills of the mediator are paramount as well as the quality of listening. We shall conclude this chapter with a few distinctions on the important subject of active listening in mediation. It is helpful to recognize that that are different levels of listening, which can be summarized as:

Hearing

Hearing is just about the physical phenomenon of 'hearing' someone's voice: you simply register that they are speaking. This is the most superficial level of listening and only requires that your ears are functioning. You do not have to pay any attention to hear people and, at this level, you will be unlikely to take on board or to remember what they have said.

Listening

Everyday listening can be more about listening to yourself than to the other person. This is 'listening', but from your own perspective while engaging with the 'mind talk' in your head and simultaneously having a conversation with yourself – asking 'what does this mean to me?', or perhaps recalling memories of when something similar happened to you, or again asking 'how do I feel about this?' or 'what's the best thing to say in this situation?'

This is adequate listening for everyday life but pretty poor on attention in respect of the person who is talking to you. This kind of listening is filtered through your own beliefs, values and experiences, and therefore often results in misconstrued assumptions about what the other person is actually saying or meaning.

Such listening – where you are rehearsing in your mind what you are going to say while the other person is still speaking – is often flawed in that while listening to your own mind talk, you cannot fully listen to what someone is saying to you. As soon as the other person takes a breath or leaves a second of space, such a 'listener' will likely jump in with what they want to say or to express their own point of view.

Listening with quality attention

This is a deeper level, a deeper quality of authentic listening and the one that is required in mediation or skilful conflict management. This kind of listening requires you to give your complete attention to the other person and what they are saying. It needs your own mind to 'shut up' and to keep quiet. It means allowing yourself to listen to what someone is saying with an open posture and an open mind: no preconceptions, no assumptions, no misguided conclusions.

This is what we mean when we refer to 'active listening with quality attention', and this is how a good mediator listens throughout the whole mediation process and to each person in the mediation. The attention is on the other person, and not on you. It is a very 'allowing' listening, letting the person say what they need to say without unnecessary interruption, without any personal agenda of your own.

It is the purest form of listening and will enable you to really hear what people are saying, what is important to them, and what the real issues are for them. Because such listening is relaxed, this ease and open-mindedness will mean that you can more effortlessly recall or summarize back the essence of what has been said.

This kind of active listening and giving good attention to another person is not only good listening but it has another very powerful effect. It appears to have a positive quality all of its own. When people are given this level of attention, say in a conflict situation or a mediation, it serves them by helping them become clearer themselves about what they are saying or their experiences. It may also help them to emotionally and mentally process it in some way – which can put them in a more resourceful place for the mediation itself.

The quality of your attention will determine the quality of the communication.

Chapter 3: The essentials

The mediator has individual meetings with each party to the mediation first and then, if they are willing, brings them together in a joint face-to-face mediation meeting. A mediation meeting is not just a 'free for all' – this face-to-face meeting is structured into six steps or stages and it is the mediation structure and the level of its confidentiality and quality of listening that contributes to the high success of mediation.

This chapter outlines and describes each of these mediation steps and also describes the mediation 'ground rules' that underpin this meeting and allows the mediator to manage the communication so that it remains as constructive as possible.

In this way, the mediator is responsible for the overall 'direction' of the mediation, while the discussions and the content of the communication within this are up to the parties themselves. As such, 'it is their problem and their solution.' The mediator then has a follow-up meeting with the parties at an agreed time in the future, in order to see how the agreements are working out. Completion of this follow-up meeting concludes the mediation.

4

Finding your way around conflict resolution:

what is special about mediation?

Having looked at the nature, principles and six-step structure of mediation we are now in a position to consider how this unique intervention differs from other forms of conflict resolution. Conflict resolution is a vast subject and covers areas as diverse as international conflict, labour and industrial disputes, community conflicts and cultural integration, domestic, marital and family court mediations and of course the subject of this book: workplace mediation.

Although these wider contexts are not directly relevant to our present investigation, it may be useful at this point to review some of the common principles of conflict resolution and also to situate mediation within the continuum of informal and formal conflict resolution methods that are available to workplace dispute and conflicts. Finally in this chapter we shall consider the question: 'What is special about mediation?'

For those who wish to go more deeply into the academic models of conflict resolution or mediation mentioned both here and in other chapters, a list of references and suggested reading appears in the bibliography at the end of this book.

THE NATURE OF 'CONFLICT'

It is interesting that the academic definition of conflict has changed over the years and that these changes reflect a shift in social and international relationships and indeed in our developing view of human nature. In the cold war era conflict was clearly centred upon matters of 'positions', 'dominance' and of 'end-games' unequivocally centred upon winning and losing. This view was based upon, and in turn reinforced, a view of human nature and motivation as essentially self-interested and selfish, and a world in which exclusive needs and resources are to be had only at the expense of others.

This attitude was interestingly reflected in the emergence of the social psychology of 'gaming research', which offered detailed working models of the chess game of individual and social self-interest. Gaming theory also provided rich paradigms and formulas for the US military, who were constantly trying to second-guess the nuclear 'end-games' of international threat and counter-threat. In this vein, then, Coser in 1976 defines conflict as 'a struggle over values and claims to scarce status, power, and resources in which the aims of the opponents are to neutralize, injure or eliminate the rivals'.

Since that time developments in social science and in humanistic and other individual psychologies have enriched our perception of human interaction and offer us a less pathological and more healthy model that extends to the 'farther reaches of human nature' and that includes altruism as a natural inherent progression of human nature and of our innate needs and values (Maslow, 1971). As a result of this expansion in thinking later definitions of conflict include new positive elements of interdependence and even allow for the possibility of conflict as a transformative route – that can lead to a better adjustment of relationships and improved joint outcomes. By 1992 for example Donohue and Kolt had come to define conflict as: 'A situation in which independent people express (manifest or latent) differences in satisfying their individual needs and interests and they experience interference from each other in accomplishing these goals'.

The new important constituent elements in this later definition can be listed and expanded as:

- underlying _'differences'_ that are acknowledged and respected;
- that are based on _'interests'_ between people who _interact_;
- and who are willing to _'invent options for mutual gain'_;
- using _'objective and not personal criteria'_.

This list summarizes in fact the improved style of US–Soviet conflict negotiation that was developed by the Harvard Negotiation Project and

captured in the two classics of interest-based conflict resolution and negotiation: *Getting to Yes* (Fisher, Ury and Patton, 1981) and *Getting Together*
(Fisher and Brown, 1989).

Essentially it can be said that conflict is ultimately about a drive for some
kind of change in the status quo. As Andrew Acland writes in *A Sudden
Outbreak of Common Sense* (1990): 'All conflict is about someone's wish for
change versus someone's resistance to change.' The evolving definition of
'conflict' opens the way to next consider in more depth the principles of
'division' and of 'unity' that operate within conflict resolution.

THE ELEMENTS THAT CAN DIVIDE

In considering what underpins conflict it is perhaps useful to take a view
of some of the core elements that can divide.

What can constitute the grounds for conflict?

Some of the variables that can divide us and generate conflict include:

- *Personal psychology.* Studies in psychology from the psychodynamic to
  humanistic and other contemporary cognitive and behavioural
  psychologies have shown us how crucial to conflict is the *perception* of
  each individual involved and how crucial are the thinking, feeling and
  behavioural patterns of each individual in the origination, escalation,
  manifestation and resolution of any conflict.
- *Group norms and psychology.* Modern social psychology indicates how
  family, social and societal norms can play a formative part in the
  origins of interpersonal and inter-group difference and in the subsequent conflict arising from group needs, norms and identities.
- *Stereotypes and prejudice.* An acute aspect of social conflict derives from
  social stereotyping and prejudice. Gordon Allport in *The Nature of
  Prejudice* (1954) provided a first and classic description of how individuals and groups come to perpetuate cultural, social, ideological or
  social divides.
- *Power.* We all share a drive towards self and group fulfilment,
  supported by our survival and aggressive urges, and directed to
  achieving the power that we need both to survive and to fulfil our
  wider and higher personal and social needs. Unequal power – especially that which denies the needs of others – clearly creates the ingredients for reaction and conflict.

THE PRINCIPLES THAT UNITE

Conflict can originate in _what divides us_. In the same way the key to _conflict resolution_ lies in understanding and putting into place _what it is that unites us_. In all effective and lasting processes of conflict resolution, the _uniting_ can be said to take place through both a 'deconstructing' and a 'reconstructing' process. We can usefully view the deconstructing elements as:

▊ _Gaining understanding through communication._ All conflict is multi-layered and has come into being through a complex and sometimes lengthy process of behaviours, events and perceptions that have escalated and become reinforced into positions and triggers for further conflict. The unfolding of conflict takes place where a _hidden_ divergence of needs, interests or values emerges or is triggered into an _open manifestation_ of argument, clashes, incidents and consequent stated and publicly held positions. The complexity of this build-up requires a careful communication process to deconstruct this tangle by first acknowledging and venting the built up feeling, and then gradually and incrementally restoring an understanding of the _nature of the differences_ and the real _issues_ that these differences represent.

▊ _Exploring interests not positions._ What makes the difference in achieving this understanding is whether the process of ventilation is limited to an emotionally driven _argument_ – which will only tend to reinforce _positions_ – or whether it is based on a fact-based process of _disclosure and feedback_ around the _experience, interests and needs_ of each of the parties involved in the conflict. It is only this latter that offers any true grounds for conflict resolution.

Deconstructing conflict then is about unravelling the complexity and about uncovering the differences in needs and interests that have come to underpin the conflict. The second element of 'reconstructing' involves:

▊ _Restoring respect._ For communication to be effective, a relationship must be established or restored that allows the parties to view each other with respect. This involves an agreement to replace the vicious circles of accusation, judgement and misinterpretation with a willingness to listen and to understand the other.

▊ _Exploring commonalities and shared ground._ Essentially the meeting ground for those in conflict is a mixture of their shared history and of their mutually frustrated, underlying needs. It is in the sharing of 'their story' and the discovery of their needs – within a process of new understanding and potential reconciliation – that the possibility can arise of *extending the shared ground* to creatively engineer *mutually beneficial* instead of damaging *unilateral* solutions.

▌ *Reframing the ground.* This involves a willingness to relinquish the focus of *difference, conflict and hurt* in favour of the will to create *behaviour-based solutions* that will satisfy *mutual needs.* This ground Fisher, Ury and Patton describe, in *Getting to Yes,* as being from 'shared interests' to shared gains.

Essentially then we could say that the principles that unite depend upon 'reframing' the ground from the 'I' to the 'We'.

This process is described by Richard E Walton – in *Interpersonal Peacemaking* (1981) – as moving from the *differentiation* that perpetuates conflict to the territory of *integration* and mutuality in which the parties can 'appreciate their similarities, acknowledge their common goals, own up to positive aspects of their ambivalence, express warmth and respect and/or engage in other positive activities to manage their conflict'.

DISPUTE RESOLUTION METHODS

We shall shift our focus in this section from the *principles of conflict resolution* to examine the spectrum of *dispute resolution methods* that are typically available to businesses and organizations when faced with the breakdown of working relationships. We shall look at the nature and characteristics of each avenue of conflict intervention before concluding with an evaluation of the special place of mediation within this continuum of dispute methods.

We shall also look briefly at what the *process and the philosophy* behind mediation has to offer to the development of business cultures and shall develop these thoughts more fully in the last chapter, 'Beyond mediation'.

There are perhaps five broad avenues of action open to an organization to manage and resolve conflict. These are: informal negotiation, mediation, conciliation, arbitration and litigation. Each of these approaches has its individual features and its own limitations.

Some of these processes are participant-led and others are usually termed third-party interventions – where the process is managed or facilitated by some source outside the conflict or by an independent or legal arbiter entrusted with the task of resolving the situation by way of a judgement and prescriptive action. In general, it is true to say that the more extensive the nature of the resolution methodologies, the less likely it is that the parties involved will achieve a solution from which all will gain. In addition the time/financial expenditure and the personal or organizational damage increases proportionately as the matter progresses from informal to formal resolution.

These methodologies are described in brief below.

Informal negotiation

This term may be taken to embrace any person-to-person interaction where participants are seeking an informal mutual agreement. They may do this simply on the basis of discussion or with some kind of agreed deal or compromise solution. This kind of negotiation is often based on bargaining whereby each person pushes for the best deal for him/herself.

This process can remain confidential by agreement and no other party needs to be involved. Sometimes, however, informal help may be offered in this process by friends, by peer group or perhaps through confidential HR, occupational health or other informal involvement.

Mediation

Mediation, as we have seen, involves an intervention whereby an impartial mediator (internal or external) is called upon to provide a structured process within which the parties can exchange understandings about their feelings and issues and can, by agreement, explore new outcomes and together create an agreement for future improvements.

This is still a confidential and informal process but has a public outcome via the voluntary agreements, which should not however appear on employee records.

Facilitation or 'facilitated dialogue'

When a situation of work conflict does not sit easily within the parameters and principles of mediation, there is still the flexible option of offering _independent facilitation_. This involves someone independent of the parties, or someone external to the organization – such as an independent consultant with appropriate skills and experience – who is invited to facilitate a meeting between those in conflict. This facilitation may not include the principles of mediation or be about working relationships and may provide a different approach to facilitated organizational communication or negotiation.

Conciliation

The escalation of unresolved conflict necessitates the involvement in the proceedings of one or more *third parties*. These agents may be line or senior managers, HR or perhaps other conciliatory bodies such as ACAS. They will basically listen to those in conflict and, having gathered sufficient information, will then assist them by offering advice and helping them move towards decisions.

Though not normally mandatory, these recommended solutions are hopefully adopted by the parties in conflict. This process of its nature is public and will probably therefore be entered on employee records.

Arbitration

This further process adds to conciliation a more formal element whereby the arbitrator, having listened to and weighed up the evidence from both sides, then adjudicates as to the best option for the restoration of performance. The resulting decision may be imposed upon the participants (if it is, for example, binding in law) or may be stated by the arbitrator to be non-binding. Here it is another authority – the arbitrator – that makes the decisions.

This process also covers decisions generated by internal business investigations, management resolutions imposed by authority or the results of a formal disciplinary hearing. These decisions are of course public and will therefore be recorded in employee records.

Litigation

This final process refers specifically to 'recourse to law', either by the employer or by the employee. This may involve variously employment tribunals and civil litigation. The process at this stage will be almost entirely out of the hands of the participants and is prosecuted or defended by lawyers on the basis of evidence submitted to court and of subsequent arguments that are then adjudicated by the judge or jury. This is a public, adversarial and binding process, and consequently there is inevitably a winner and a loser.

In real terms, however, there can often be multiple losers in such situations, simply in terms of the financial and emotional costs to those taking part – as well as damage to reputations or to future employment prospects of the parties involved in the dispute.

A COMPARATIVE CONTINUUM OF WORKPLACE INTERVENTIONS

Figure 4.1 shows the processes of conflict resolution described above as a comparative continuum of interventions. It will be clear from this diagram that the least formal and most participant-controlled processes offer the greatest self-determination, the most significant gains and the least damage. By contrast the most formal and the least participant-controlled interventions are, by their nature, the most public, lengthy, costly and damaging, and are the least likely to deliver an outcome that is mutually acceptable or a win to all parties.

Comparative and evaluative criteria for conflict resolution

- the earlier or later timing of the conflict intervention;
- the locus of control and accountability involved for those in conflict;
- the informal or formal status of the process used;
- the conciliatory or punitive nature of the resulting outcomes;
- the private/confidential versus public/recorded nature of the proceedings;
- the level of cost – whether financial, personal or in terms of attrition to the business or to personal reputation and credibility;
- the overall results that extend from, at best, a mutual win–win through a win–lose to, at worst, a lose–lose outcome extending to all those involved.

WHAT IS SPECIAL ABOUT MEDIATION?

It will be apparent from this brief summary of dispute resolution methods that mediation has a particular value as a tool of choice for conflict resolution. In terms of the criteria shown in the box above, mediation can be said to be a unique and positive process that can be characterized as beneficial in all the following ways:

- Mediation offers a conflict resolution process that can be suggested and adopted at a very early point in a conflict or dispute.
- Mediation offers the fullest possible involvement of the participants in the control, accountability and determination of the positive outcome of the event.

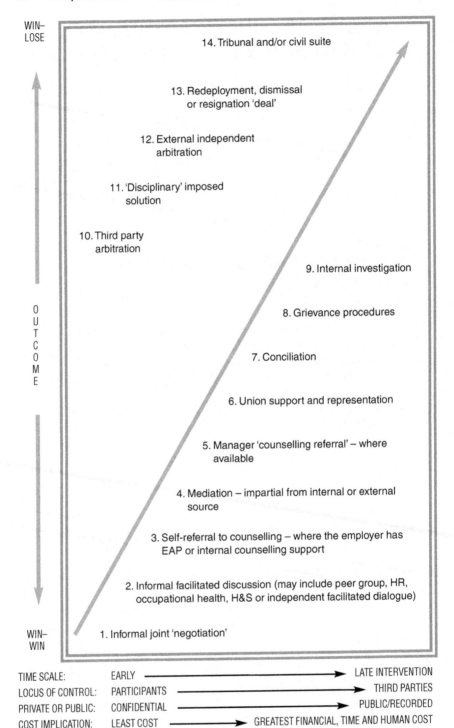

WIN–LOSE

14. Tribunal and/or civil suite

13. Redeployment, dismissal or resignation 'deal'

12. External independent arbitration

11. 'Disciplinary' imposed solution

10. Third party arbitration

9. Internal investigation

8. Grievance procedures

7. Conciliation

6. Union support and representation

5. Manager 'counselling referral' – where available

4. Mediation – impartial from internal or external source

3. Self-referral to counselling – where the employer has EAP or internal counselling support

2. Informal facilitated discussion (may include peer group, HR, occupational health, H&S or independent facilitated dialogue)

1. Informal joint 'negotiation'

WIN–WIN

OUTCOME

TIME SCALE:	EARLY	LATE INTERVENTION
LOCUS OF CONTROL:	PARTICIPANTS	THIRD PARTIES
PRIVATE OR PUBLIC:	CONFIDENTIAL	PUBLIC/RECORDED
COST IMPLICATION:	LEAST COST	GREATEST FINANCIAL, TIME AND HUMAN COST

Figure 4.1 Comparative place of mediation in 'conflict resolution' methods

▊ Mediation remains an informal and confidential process – though the outcome agreement is lodged publicly (but 'off-record') with the employer.

▊ Mediation is highly cost-effective in terms of the immediate renewal of performance and the restoration of working relationships and job satisfaction.

▊ Mediation is financially advantageous when compared to the time and financial costs of other more protracted or third-party-based solutions.

▊ Mediation is also vastly advantageous when compared with the financial and time-based involvement that attaches to legal action for resolving disputes.

▊ Finally and overall, mediation offers uniquely the most significant chance of multiple win–win outcomes for all the participants, as well as for their business or organization. Mediation can be said to give people the opportunity for their 'real' needs to be met.

▊ As such mediation also contributes to the morale and emotional health of any organizations that choose to give it pride of place in their conflict resolution culture.

In essence then, mediation offers a methodology that is significantly different from conventional processes and norms in the workplace.

Chapter 4: The essentials

We began this chapter with an overview of the principles that underlie the extensive field of conflict resolution. We noted the evolution of the definitions of conflict from the wholly negative 'struggle for resources' to the possibility that 'conflicting differences in interdependent relationships' – if approached positively and handled creatively – can actually result in improved relationships and shared gains. Such an evolution of thought is significant in that it transforms the _problem_ of conflict into the _opportunity for creative difference_.

We looked more deeply at the elements that divide within conflict and at the 'principles that unite' that help to restore relationships and to promote the _integration_ necessary in the transition from the 'I' to the 'We'.

In the second half of this chapter we looked at the range of contemporary tools available for conflict resolution in the workplace and described how workplace mediation differs from other forms of dispute resolution – negotiation, conciliation, facilitated 'dialogue', arbitration and litigation.

Mediation is unique and is significantly different in that it is structured, has a third-party facilitator (the mediator) and is based on win–win mutual solutions and agreements that remain in the hands of those involved.

As a process, mediation has much to recommend it in terms of efficiency, employee empowerment and cost effectiveness. As a model of empowerment and self-determination it provides a powerful example of how organizational and business cultures can maximize their human assets and potential.

5

How mediation can be used within organizations

In this chapter we shall explore how mediation can be used in support of, and as a part of, people management and people policies at work. Starting with a look at the measure of relationship breakdown, we shall examine at what point mediation may become viable, who needs to instigate or manage the process and how mediation can be used informally or formally within personnel policies and in other wider contexts such as customer complaints systems.

MEDIATION WHEN WORKING RELATIONSHIPS BREAK DOWN

The starting place for the use of mediation is when people at work are just not getting on with each other. Typically, reasons for the breakdown of relationships can include those shown in the box below.

Reasons for the breakdown of relationships

I Personality clashes: people just do not like each other, cannot work together.
I Different expectations of management or communication styles.
I Resentments and grudges building up to such an extent they begin to negatively affect how people cooperate or work together.
I Different values or 'maps' of reality formed from each individual's personal history, experiences and beliefs.
I Personal aggression, with someone attempting to 'get at the other' in a punitive way. This can manifest in many ways, from a mild dislike right through to harassment or bullying behaviours or downright prejudice. Aggression can also be indirect and can take the more passive/aggressive route of attempting to harm others or their reputation or even their job by means of lodging spurious complaints or by creating alliances against them.

Understandably in all this, there is a continuum in the seriousness of the conflict that bears a direct relationship to the likelihood of a successful resolution. The less serious the breakdown and the quicker it is addressed, the more likely there will be a speedy and mutually satisfactory resolution. By contrast, it follows that the more a conflict is left unmanaged or unresolved, the more likely it is to develop into a stressful and costly situation for all concerned and the more likely also that it will spread and will involve others – such as colleagues or team members.

Interpersonal conflicts can manifest in the workplace in many ways, including those shown below. All of these create interpersonal and performance problems, especially if members are supposed to be working directly together or in a direct line management position to each other.

Manifestations of interpersonal conflict

These include:

I *direct outbursts* of aggression, anger or upset;
I attempts to make *alliances with others*, to get them on one's side – including the *use of 'gossip'* to undermine and disparage the other;
I *poor or ineffective communication*, a general lack of communication or consultation, abrupt or unfriendly ways of communicating with each

other, avoidance of each other, 'put downs' of the other person or of his/her suggestions and ideas, and finally simply not talking to each other at all;

■ indirect 'non-cooperation', involving the passive/aggressive blocking of the other with 'power plays' and other forms of 'games', 'dramas' or ritualized conflicts.

The growing effects of such conflicts are variously visible in work terms in:

■ *Poor work performance.* In terms of quality of work or service; problems with work distribution, poor decision making; lack of initiative/creativity; more likelihood of poor judgement or accidents at work.

■ *Increased absenteeism.* In all its forms, from coming in late or just disappearing for a while to long-term sickness absence due to stress or ill health.

■ *Increased number of complaints.* These may be matched by decreasing morale and high staff turnover.

■ *Failing management.* Where the conflict involves a breakdown within a line management situation, then this may show up in increasing avoidance by managers, inadequate or unsatisfactory supervision and appraisal of staff through to a full breakdown in lines of communication.

Is any of the above familiar? If you have ever worked in an organization or have yourself been in a position of managing people, it is most likely that you will have had some experience of such situations or witnessed such conflicts. It is abundantly clear that interpersonal breakdowns in the workplace can be very damaging indeed. If left unchecked or unmanaged, these kinds of conflicts can increase in complexity and take up a huge amount of time and energy, a 'hidden cost' that most organizations can well do without.

So where does mediation come into all this?

MEDIATION AS AN INFORMAL RESOLUTION WITHIN PERSONNEL POLICIES

There are basically two levels of intervention possible when working relationships begin to break down: the everyday and the formal levels.

The everyday conflict management level

When conflicts are less serious and no formal complaint has been made, it is basically up to the line managers to manage the situation so as to resolve the problem and do all they can to encourage their staff to work well together. This means that managers need to have the conflict resolution skills to de-escalate conflicts between their staff as they arise in the course of everyday working life. Some of these skills we shall examine in more detail in Chapter 13, where we offer managers some key conflict resolution formats, including the Brief Mediation™ model.

Equally, managers may decide to manage the situation through individual or team meetings with those involved. Managing such meetings productively, so they achieve the results required, calls for quite a high level of effective group communication and conflict management skills.

The formal level

This is reached when conflicts escalate and one or both parties to the conflict put in a formal grievance or a complaint through personnel policies such as harassment and bullying, dignity at work, equal opportunities and so on. It is not unusual for these kinds of interpersonal work conflicts to end up with one person putting in a complaint and the other party retaliating by putting in a counter-complaint or appealing – thus making the dispute both more complex and drawn out.

Of course, personnel policies do have an important place in dealing formally with conflicts and workplace complaints. However, these procedures are not designed, nor are they suitable, for adequately dealing with volatile relationship conflicts with all their strong feelings and personal complications. Nor are they usually helpful in fully satisfying the needs of the parties around being heard, acknowledged and understood. Organizational procedures in fact often themselves precipitate an unnecessary escalation of the problem.

Clearly, it is the ultimate responsibility of the managers to manage their staff. However, in situations of strong interpersonal conflict, then it is likely that managers will share their appraisal of the situation – and any decision on the appropriateness of mediation – with their line managers or with human resources. Both managers and HR practitioners therefore need to have a clear understanding of the nature of mediation and the role that it can play in the resolution of conflict.

Increasingly we are finding that mediation is being written into the personnel policies of organizations and this is where it is most used. In

Chapter 14 we shall return to the place of mediation within the continuum of conflict resolution interventions open to a business or organization.

Different organizations have different policies, but mediation is now being written into policies that deal with working relations such as grievance, harassment and bullying, dignity or respect at work, equal opportunities, disability or age discrimination, equality and diversity, and gender recognition rulings.

In line with what has been said about the seriousness and progression of conflict, mediation is best situated as a first stage of informal, confidential resolution within these kinds of policies. Equally, however, mediation can also be utilized as the last or final intervention when formal investigation has found 'no' or 'insufficient' evidence of guilt. At this last stage, mediation can be recommended or offered in order to help re-build working relationships between those involved or between those affected, which can involve a team mediation.

Another interesting alternative that some organizations are choosing is that of writing a stand-alone mediation or dispute resolution policy. There are many benefits to this. A separate mediation policy can outline more clearly what situations are appropriate for mediation, how mediation can be accessed by employees, the timings and confidentiality rules, and roles and responsibilities.

The other advantage of a separate mediation policy is that it can make mediation and constructive dispute resolution more usable and more accessible to staff so that conflicts can be more positively resolved before they escalate. People may, in time, feel more able to flag up problems if they know there is a more positive, fair, confidential way of sorting them out. It can also mean that people are more willing to go for mediation rather than go through the more stressful formal personnel approaches.

The recent rapid growth in mediation has a lot to do with the fact that organizations, private or public, are being encouraged to deal with complaints and disputes with their own internal dispute resolution procedures before going to employment tribunals. The UK government, in particular, is encouraging 'constructive dialogue' and the use of such measures as mediation or other appropriate dispute resolution methods for employee disputes and complaints as part of the statutory dispute resolution changes that came into force in October 2004. These changes have since been reviewed and developed within the recommendations of the Gibbons Report in 2007.

The new directives for resolving work disputes are there to encourage employers and employees to discuss problems first, before going to an employment tribunal. So much so, that both the organization and the individual employee can both be financially penalized by an employment tribunal if they have not first used these internal strategies. In response to this, many organizations are arranging for external mediation by independent mediation companies, or alternatively they are choosing to establish their own 'internal mediation service' with all the training and coordination that this entails (see Chapter 8).

Most of the mediations carried out at the moment come under this first stage of a personnel policy. If people agree to resolve by mediation, then the sooner it is carried out the better. This informal first stage of a policy enables parties to communicate with each other and find ways of resolving through a confidential mediation meeting, facilitated by a skilled and experienced mediator.

As we have said earlier, mediation is about agreements and solutions that will improve the working relationship rather than destroy it. So, for those who agree to go through the mediation process, the majority experience a successful outcome. It is commonly agreed amongst professional mediators that there is an average of an 80 per cent to 90 per cent success rate, which is pretty high whichever way you look at it.

This means that while not all employee disputes are suitable for mediation, a significantly large percentage of complaints can be successfully dealt with by early mediation intervention. It is also important to point out that if the dispute is too serious in nature, then it would *not* be appropriate to offer mediation and the case would go straight into a formal investigation.

MEDIATION AFTER A FORMAL INVESTIGATION HAS TAKEN PLACE

As can be imagined, where a formal investigation has been carried out (with possible suspension of those involved and colleagues interviewed) and it ends with 'no fault found' or 'insufficient evidence', the situation and the feelings of those involved will have escalated almost beyond recognition and will now be affecting more people in the team or from different management layers.

At this point both the complainant and the one complained about may well feel very betrayed and dissatisfied with both the process and the organization. Often they feel that, for all the upset and disruption that they have been through, nothing has substantially changed. Neither party in this situation feels vindicated or acknowledged and moreover their issues, around working together, still remain.

Offering these two hurt and angry people mediation at this stage, after all they have been through, is evidently not the best of timing. Obviously, an early mediation, when no formal complaint has been made or at the first stage of a complaint through a personnel policy, is going to be far easier and have a better chance of succeeding than a mediation that takes place after a formal investigation.

Having said that, however, there is still a place for mediation at this later stage – keeping in mind that the heightened feelings and entrenched reactions of those involved will most probably mean it will be more difficult or more demanding of the mediator and of those taking part in the mediation.

If a formal investigation has taken place, and there were insufficient facts to prove anyone was guilty of anything, then the reality remains that these two people still have a problem. Given that people still have to work together after an investigation, many investigators are now recommending mediation as part of their investigation conclusions.

At this stage other colleagues and team members, more likely than not, will also have been embroiled in the conflict and will have their own feelings and difficulties surrounding it. So, frequently, two mediations will actually take place at this later stage: one between the two parties involved and then a further one between the parties and their full team. Many times during such mediations, participants have said how much they wished mediation could have been offered right at the beginning as it could have saved them much heartache and emotional distress.

MEDIATION AS PART OF YOUR CUSTOMER OR CLIENT COMPLAINTS PROCEDURE

Adopting mediation as a part of your client or customer complaints procedures is very similar to mediation used as a first stage of a personnel policy except that, in this case, it is the first stage of a complaints policy. In both policies, the complainant and those complained about are both given the opportunity to talk through their difficulties and the chance to find the solutions they would be satisfied with. The aims and principles of mediation remain the same. If the mediation proves unsuccessful and agreement cannot be reached, then legal processes can be instigated.

Such an arrangement provides the chance for the necessary communication to take place for there to be some kind of simpler resolution, as opposed to the cost and time involved in legal action. Some specific examples where mediation has become a part of complaints procedures include those listed in the box below. While the main aim of workplace mediation is to improve working relationships, mediation for these types of complaints can result in a number of other possible outcome agreements, including financial compensation. In these kinds of cases, all the stake-holders involved need to be present in the mediation meeting. For instance, a mediation involving compensation to a patient would also include the presence of the person/s within the hospital trust who can make such financial decisions as well as legal professionals.

Areas where complaints may be resolved by mediation

I user complaints within, for example, social services, local authorities, and charities;
I patient complaints within the National Health Service;
I financial, insurance or ombudsman schemes;
I police, probation and the prison service;
I housing associations, service complaints or tenant disputes;
I consumer/customer complaints;
I schools and education.

Also, it can be seen within medical complaints, that the opportunity for frank and honest discussions and communication within mediation can help, for instance, a patient or family of a patient to hear directly from the medical staff concerned with an explanation of what actually happened. This kind of communication can play a large part in helping people come to some understanding and possibly to some kind of closure, and it is this kind of communication that is not usually offered by formal or legal procedures.

The advantages can be many, not only in emotional or financial terms but also in terms of time – mediation can help resolve matters much more quickly than going through lawyers and court proceedings. Best of all for all parties involved, mediation remains a voluntary process with mutu-ally agreed outcomes even within complaints policies.

Organizations that adopt mediation for employee disputes, often also adopt it as part of their complaints procedures as a 'whole organizational' approach to the resolution of conflicts.

As regards the legal status of agreements, workplace mediation is a 'non-binding' process within workplace relationships. It is confidential, voluntary and 'without prejudice', which means it cannot later be used in a court or any other formal or legal proceedings. For formal user or consumer complaints, however, a signed mediation agreement can be made legally enforceable, and therefore legally binding, if both parties agree to this.

There will be times when mediation makes a lot of sense, and there will also be times when pursuing complaints through formal means and the courts is the necessary option.

Chapter 5: The essentials

The more conflict is left unmanaged or unresolved or festering, the more likely it is to develop into a costly and stressful situation for all concerned. In this chapter we cover some of the reasons why working relations break down, but it is clear that complex interpersonal disputes can take up a huge amount of time and energy that might better be employed elsewhere.

While formal investigations are necessary and have their place, they can sometimes make the situation worse and can end up causing great anxiety and stress, with neither party getting what they want.

The majority of mediations take place as a voluntary first stage of both personnel and customer complaints policies, though they are also carried out after formal investigations have taken place to help disputing parties continue working together.

The advantages of mediation are many, not only in terms of emotional and financial cost, but it is also much quicker to set up and is based on supporting and rebuilding the working relationship rather than destroying it.

6

Workplace mediation for teams

Anyone who has worked in an organization recognizes the negative impact of unresolved or festering conflicts within a team. There are team members who do not get on or who avoid working together; there is the damaging gossip; there are teams who work to undermine their managers; there can be backbiting and downright denigration of others; sometimes there are alliances and sub-groups, with those who are 'in' and those who are 'out', and perhaps a manager or team leader who does not know how to manage or to challenge team members effectively.

Such situations will often end up with some kind of eruption of frayed tempers, or some 'incident' will occur and formal complaints such as a grievance or bullying complaint or threatened resignations go flying into the human resources department. Individuals in the team often go off work with stress-related illness at such times and the work of the team, as well as its morale, can suffer severely as a result.

Whilst it is possible for teams to develop multiple problems, it is equally true that the team is currently enjoying a growing importance in business and organizational life. This phenomenon has even assumed a heroic proportion, born out of the Japanese post-war drive for quality, continuous improvement and customer-driven accountability that centred upon the pivotal unit of the work team. These developments that marked the Japanese economic resurgence also fuelled derivative US and

European team models, and the work team is now acknowledged as a key business and organizational resource.

Understanding team conflicts, making the decision to offer mediation, understanding ways to organize a team mediation all involve some level of complexity, which is why in this chapter we will be outlining all these team factors in some detail.

SO WHAT LIES BEHIND TEAM CONFLICT?

Teams are formed by functional groupings of employees with a spread of roles, expertise, experience and interdependence. Teams are, therefore, to some extent, somewhat like the people that inhabit them. They have a personality, a flavour and a mix that can vary and that can change and evolve. Teams, like individuals, also have their own psychological and behavioural dynamics and go through their own cycles of evolution and development.

A number of things can unbalance a team or can make for temporary or longer-term problems such as division, differences and conflict. There are many precipitators of team dysfunction. We shall survey some of these briefly and then look at some situational scenarios that the mediator may typically be called in to address.

Team composition

The blend of the people making up a work or organizational team gives it a special flavour and a level of cohesion and effectiveness that can change or be threatened as the team composition changes. There have been numerous psychological attempts to categorize and to provide formulas to describe team composition and balance. Perhaps the best known, in the business context, is the Myers Briggs Type Indicator (MBTI), with its delineation of typologies based upon personality traits and its implications for the effects of the group mix on team performance.

Given that teams do not exist in a laboratory and that they cannot be constituted and re-balanced on a permanent basis, then some of these descriptions remain interesting but academic. What is important for the team leader and for the mediator working with teams, is to acquire the ability to recognize the temperamental and psychological differences that go to make up the current blend of their team and to be aware that, as the team composition changes, so the blend, profile and output of the team will likely change as well.

Teams and change

Organizational and working changes can all translate as threats to the 'team personality' and such perceived threats can, in their turn, originate conflict. New team members, new managers, new team leaders, new organizational changes or changes in working conditions or corporate style can all affect and destabilize a team and create stresses and tensions that reduce team cohesiveness and effectiveness.

Change management is a vast subject but, in essence, if change is prescribed from the top – in terms of the goals *and* the means – then teams will have little to engage with. Unless the team happens to share identical goals and would choose the identical means, they are likely to regard unilateral organizational changes as anything from irritating to marginalizing, directly threatening or at worst destructive of their interests and values. The effects of poor change management are sadly all too common; they are the cause of much team-based resentment or cynicism and can lead to overt or covert reactive undermining or conflict.

Sometimes this unsettlement is directed towards team managers or team leaders – especially if they are new to the group or are still establishing their authority in a 'command and control' business culture. They may also become a psychological 'target' as teams project their fears or their displaced anxiety onto the 'parent' role that managers can assume.

Team relationships

Most typically, team conflicts are more parochial than corporate in nature, and may revolve around the dynamics of personalities and of temperamental clashes or mismatches. A psychological feature that is more prevalent in groups is conflict arising from social, class or racial stereotyping and discrimination. The group dimension of a random, cross-functional, multi-skilled group can give prejudices more room to emerge and can generate conflicts that would be less likely to occur in natural or chosen social groupings.

Conversely, it is also true that some teams have very close pre-existing social groupings, so that a work team may contain several extended family members, a number of members from a particular village or urban district, or perhaps a group that regularly socializes or engages in shared sports, pastimes, clubs, pubs or social and political groupings.

Will Shutz in *The Human Element* (1994) says: 'Teams perform to their potential only when members accept themselves, take responsibility for their feelings and interact constructively with others.' He also recognizes that different types of work cultures in an organization can have a direct effect on the kind of relationships and conflicts that can arise within a team. The atmospheres that form the bases for team decision making and relational interaction he defined by the work cultures of Inclusion, Control and Openness. These are useful parameters for profiling inter-active team dynamics and can be shown schematically as in the box below.

INCLUSION – *to do with the level of contact in a team, or the group versus individual work*

HIGH –	Lots of contact, frequent meetings, lots of interpersonal interaction.
LOW –	Low contact: people hardly see each other, separate offices or out of the office a lot, mainly do own individual tasks.
CONFLICT:	Some members want to solve problems by meeting and talking and doing things as a team, others want to solve them through getting on with their individual job with little reference to others.

CONTROL – *to do with the amount of control and structure in a team or organization*

HIGH –	Clear, hierarchical structures, with expectation that the manager leads by giving orders.
LOW –	Minimal hierarchy or flat management structure, creative, laissez faire and more involvement with decision making.
CONFLICT:	Some people want a clear structure and everything planned out ahead, while others want a more open, less structured approach, with involvement in the decision making.

OPENNESS – *to do with the expression of feelings and more personal communication*

HIGH –	Expression of feelings, openness and honesty about what is going on, more personal communication (will need a no-blame culture for this to exist).
LOW –	No discussion of personal feelings or fears; people only communicate about work/business with no mention of feelings.
CONFLICT:	Some want things to be out in the open and to discuss their feelings and what is going on in their work relationships, while others do not want to discuss anything personal and just want to get on with the job or keep discussions to work facts and processes only.

Power and territory

Teams are groups and can sometimes exhibit the nature of tribes or clans in terms of their behaviours and attitudes towards the outside – and in relation to the 'territory' that they define as their own. One way that a group self-defines is against the others and it may be that conflict can arise from the differentiation, competition or ownership exhibited by groups as a demonstration of their power, reach, influence, status or superior effectiveness.

Some of this natural group bonding, solidarity and group striving can be beneficial to motivation, to shared endeavour and to corporate identification in the market place. However, where these instincts turn in on themselves, then group competitive characteristics may well transform into demarcation, rivalry, narrow functionalism, or at worst inter-group obstruction and conscious or unconscious sabotage.

CONFLICT SCENARIOS: HOW WILL TEAM DYSFUNCTION BE MANIFEST?

Given the above generalizations about teams and team dynamics we can ask: 'How will teams typically present to the manager, the mediator or the HR internal consultant who is called to address team conflicts or performance problems?' The scenarios shown opposite (Boxes 1–4) may help suggest how team dysfunction can manifest across the range of everyday team life.

It is at these sorts of points of conflict that the organization is forced to do something and to look carefully at the options available to them that can remedy such interpersonal dysfunctions. Team mediation is certainly an option worth considering and it is important to be clear about what team mediation is and what it is not.

TEAM MEDIATION IS NOT AN 'AWAY DAY'

It is interesting sometimes when discussing the possibility of a team mediation for team members to respond with something like – 'Oh we tried that and it didn't work... In fact it made things worse!' – only to reveal, on further enquiry, that what they identify as a 'mediation' was in fact a 'team away day' or a 'team development event'.

1. Team composition

- A new person joins an established work team and becomes the 'outsider'. The members of the established team can malign and judge this person who is made the 'scapegoat' of the group, possibly reflecting or deflecting tensions from elsewhere.
- People in the organization want to 'get someone out' – so they encourage complaints and dissent within their team or amongst other managers.
- Private and social dynamics around members' personal history, which can include friendships and relationships outside the work environment (including romantic liaisons) can have effects on their working relations or the rest of the team.
- Stereotypical assumptions about a person (which can be based on anything the group feels is 'different'), possibly racist, sexist, or issues around disability (both physical and mental) leading to a person feeling that they are being treated 'differently' from others in the team – lack of cooperation or even open confrontation. These kinds of assumptions can also include gender differences and requests to do inappropriate tasks, or different views about dress code or about what is acceptable or polite behaviour within the group norm.

2. Team relationships and communications

- Interpersonal dislike, differences, power struggles.
- Temperamental or work style clashes.
- Lack of trust (possibly as a result of past history or certain incidents).
- Over-critical, derogatory or abusive language.
- Talking about people behind their backs; damaging gossip.
- One or both persons refusing to communicate at all with the other.
- Unequal work distribution or perception of unequal treatment.
- The consequence, stress and strong feelings around formal complaints and investigations that have taken place that can often leave people feeling very hurt and betrayed. This can result in a deep lack of trust.

3. Team power, territory and history

- A member of an established group is promoted as supervisor/ manager of the group and conflict emerges – often strong personal conflicts and feelings of betrayal, 'how dare she/he lord it over us', lack of acknowledgement of the manager's/supervisor's authority, sub-groups of people form as they take sides... and so on.
- Specific incidents that cause the conflict, which can spiral into strong dislike, blocking or non-cooperative behaviour, lack of support, power plays, escalating into not talking to each other, not working together in a professional or respectful manner.
- These incidents can be of many kinds, including being told off or criticized in front of colleagues, issues of illness or specific needs, not getting promotion or holiday requirements, or a feeling of being treated 'differently' from the rest of the team or without due respect.
- The consequence of past history such as when they worked together in another team or for another organization.

4. Corporate culture, manager style and change

- General lack of effective communication.
- Differing corporate and managerial and communication styles.
- Lack of consultation, participation and control (especially around changes or new organizational procedures).
- Deliberate withholding of information or manipulation.
- Ineffective supervision or performance management.
- A new manager coming in to whom the team takes a dislike – regards him or her as ineffective (not knowing as much as other people in the team) or too dominant and bullying (possibly when attempting to effect unwelcome changes) – or they compare the new manager with their 'much liked' previous manager. Conflict can emerge strongly as team members attempt to get rid of this new person and there can be a number of formal complaints made against the manager by the team.
- Or the other way round: new members of the team, maybe young and up and coming 'management material', find their team manager outdated, too old or ineffectual or overly autocratic in management style; power plays may come about around authority issues. Or the manager feels threatened by this new blood and can deliberately not support them to do well.

Clearly there are a broad variety of team development, training and facilitation formats currently available and being widely used – sometimes with more or less understanding of the specific goals and the dynamics and effects of these tools. Such events are mostly open-ended formats in which team issues, planning or creativity are promoted through discussion, projective techniques, team exercises or group activities.

Away days however are not, in our opinion, usually the best way to approach, or deal with team conflict – especially if conflict has become embedded or historic. The main reason for saying this is that in situations of overt or latent conflict, open-ended formats will most likely encourage the sorts of expression and interaction that are emotionally and instinctually led, that fuel dispute, disagreement or 'positions' and that can degenerate into a series of anecdotal accusations or post mortems.

Team events that attempt to deal with deep conflicts without the structure and the 'holding' of mediation often end up with people expressing their hurts and feelings and then having nowhere to go with them and no means of processing these feelings towards any change or solution. It is not surprising then that such informal airing of hidden or overt conflicts may, in fact, 'make things worse' and also render those involved more likely to shy away from such issues in the future – as they now come to associate them with unresolved tensions, outbursts, arguments and emotional scenes that they have found hard to handle.

This may be also true for the managers or team leaders involved. A manager may well have set out to facilitate a productive team discussion that is then sabotaged or threatened by the emergence of such conflict. The manager or team leader may end up having to 'referee' a team dispute or worse may decide that his/her duty is to take managerial responsibility for judging and resolving the problems now presented by the team – with the risk of earning the resentment of all concerned.

By contrast mediation is a structured and targeted process that is specifically designed to address team conflict productively and to achieve both transformative and creative change resulting in lasting agreements for the better for all those involved. In this next section we shall look in detail at both the definition and the description of the team mediation.

WHAT IS TEAM MEDIATION?

In its most simple form, team mediation is a structured mediation between a group of people. A team could be three people or anything up to 30 or more, and usually includes the direct manager/s of the team. Team mediation can be used for conflicts and differences occurring in any group of people working together in an organization, including work teams, project teams, sections, departments, senior management teams, right up to the board of directors.

Definition of team mediation

Team mediation is a structured process whereby an impartial mediator facilitates communication between a number of people in order to clarify the issues between them and to encourage them to come up with mutually beneficial solutions and agreements that will improve their working relationship in the future.

As you can see from the box, the definition and the principles are the same for team mediation as they are for a mediation between two individuals. The team mediation remains a structured dispute resolution method (following the six steps of mediation) and the mediators act as impartial facilitators with the overall aim of the improvement of working relations within the team.

The six-step structure of mediation and the principles of mediation have been described in detail in Chapters 1 and 3. Understandably, this six-step structure needs to be adapted to a larger number of participants, and there are many ways of doing this. Overall, however, the six stages, the basic structure of mediation, remain the same for team mediation. Equally a key factor in team mediation, as in all mediations, is that each member of the team needs to agree to a mediation, or at least to give it a try.

In the sections that follow, we shall look at how to set up a typical team mediation: choosing the mediators, informing and getting agreement from all the team, and arranging the team mediation day in such a way as to create the necessary conditions for a favourable outcome.

WHO SHOULD FACILITATE A TEAM MEDIATION?

Whilst most meditations between two individuals are carried out by one solo mediator, the task of mediating the complex and numerous issues and interpersonal conflicts within a team requires two mediators to hold the process and dynamics of the group. The added complexity and the prospect of highly charged emotions also mean that the mediators need to have a high level of experience in carrying out team mediation.

Mediating a team of people is no easy task and should not be taken on by newly trained mediators. We would go a little further and also say that team mediation necessitates not only excellent mediation skills but also that the mediators need to have particular training in team mediation, in dealing with strong emotions and in how to deal with the dynamics of a group.

Another reason that two mediators are necessary for team mediation is that there are more people and more conflicts present within a team, and the second mediator may be needed to do different tasks whilst the first continues to facilitate the group. For instance, during a team mediation, when someone leaves the room because of strong feelings and needs support, then one mediator may need to go out with and accompany that person. Alternatively when something unforeseen crops up, one of the mediators may need to make some phone calls or do some additional organizing in and around the mediation.

Where there are particular issues within the group – such as gender or race – then it may well be helpful for the two mediators to reflect this in order to keep the mediation a fair and equal process for everyone. For instance, it may be appropriate to have a male and female co-mediating or two mediators from different cultural backgrounds as long as they maintain their impartiality and model equal and respectful ways of working together.

There are different models of how mediators work together. For instance, some companies have a lead mediator and an assistant mediator, or a mediator and a scribe to take notes, or an experienced mediator and a trainee. We advocate a model of co-mediation for teams whereby the mediators are equal: equal experience, equal responsibility and equal airtime, facilitating the whole mediation process together, from beginning to end.

This form of 'equal co-mediation' really does have a powerful effect, as it models the very principles of mediation in action. The group will see and be influenced by two mediators who work well together in a respectful and equal way, and who remain calm and open even when feelings and tensions are running high.

Mediators collaborating together in this way can 'hold' the group, contain disturbing emotions and reactions, and gently ease the group to a more cooperative place. In this way, the two mediators model the behaviours most associated with the qualities of mediation: equality, fairness, transparency and cooperative, collaborative working.

At its best co-mediation can be like an intricate dance as the two mediators weave seamlessly in and out of leading or supporting each other and the group – with the underlying and essential aim of helping the team achieve improvements in their work practices and working relationships.

In summary, team mediation requires two co-mediators and they need to:

- be highly experienced mediators or receive specific additional training in workplace mediation for teams;
- have particular skills in dealing with strong emotions and group dynamics;
- know how to work together in an 'equal co-mediation' way;
- reflect gender or diversity issues within the group when appropriate;
- retain impartiality at all times.

WHEN TEAM MEDIATION SHOULD BE CONSIDERED AND WHEN NOT

There are a number of important considerations that go with the selection of mediation in the resolution of team difficulties and disputes. Some of these are to do with the history and processes involved and some depend upon group and individual interpersonal relationships. The box below gives a comprehensive check-list of the criteria that indicate that a team mediation is suitable or not.

Team mediation should be considered:

- when there are interpersonal issues between members of a team involving more than two people and affecting the whole team or affecting the work of the team or of the business;
- when people are not working well together or in fact avoid each other or refuse to work together;
- when one or more people put in a grievance or bullying complaint against colleagues or a manager or there are counter-complaints;
- when there are multiple conflicting issues within the team;
- when there are different subsets of conflicts, with different people not getting on for one reason or another;
- when conflicts or personal differences are affecting productivity or the quality of work or the quality of care of customers/clients/patients;

- when team conflicts or dysfunctions increase the risk of poor decision making, affect the safety of individuals or cause a higher occurrence of accidents at work;
- when the team is not working at its best, where there is a lack of cooperation or lack of proactiveness, a certain lethargy in the team and how it operates together;
- when there is a breakdown in communication such as people not communicating with each other or only communicating with each other infrequently;
- where there is the problem of inappropriate communication including disrespectful language being used, offensive jokes, memos, e-mails and so on;
- when there is a lot of destructive gossip or sub-groups or sub-alliances working against each other;
- when power struggles become destructive to the team and its goals and aims, or destructive to the organization or its success or survival as a whole;
- when individuals in the team are 'over competitive' with each other in a detrimental way;
- when there is an usually high sickness absence or staff turnover;
- when team meetings either are not well attended or do not work well or do not happen at all;
- when 'team decision making' feels obstructed in some way;
- where there is confusion or non-compliance with work practices or work guidelines;
- when there are pervasive feelings of frustration, actual 'outbursts of anger or aggression', or unfriendly or abusive language;
- when the team acts against one individual for no clear reason, where 'scapegoating' is taking place;
- when there is a bullying work culture within the team or one or more persons is acting in an abrupt or intimidating manner;
- when the team have lost confidence in their manager but there is no evidence to consider dismissal of the manager.

Team mediation should not be considered:

- when the issues are between two individuals in the team, that is, two colleagues or one team member and the manager, and do not involve the rest of the team;
- when the manager or a number of team members are not in agreement with a mediation as a means of resolving their difficulties;

- when the grievance or bullying complaints are too serious and require formal or disciplinary action;
- when there are issues of criminal activity or gross misconduct;
- when there are other formal, legal or appeal processes going on that would undermine the mediation (these would need to be all fully processed and completed or suspended before a team mediation can take place);
- when bringing people together would only increase the risk of someone being 're-abused' or 'scapegoated' in some way;
- when the team individuals or the organization are only agreeing to a mediation to show they have 'agreed to a mediation' (ie, to show evidence of this to an employment tribunal or other legal process) and not because they want to work out agreements and find a way forward for everyone in the team;
- when the issues are not 'team' issues and are outside of the remit or responsibility of the team or their manager, and they are to do with wider organizational issues.

ORGANIZING A TEAM MEDIATION

Finding experienced team mediators

Usually the first stage in setting up the team mediation is to decide on who will carry it out. This means talking to your internal mediation service or contacting an independent mediation company that is experienced in doing workplace team mediations.

Because of the added complexity of team mediation, it is important when choosing your mediators to make sure that they have several years of experience in carrying out team mediations, and in particular that they are professionally trained in team mediation and that they specialize or work in the field of workplace mediation rather than other more unrelated commercial or community sectors.

Once you have chosen who will conduct the mediation, it is important to talk through the situation with them in confidence so they can help you decide if mediation is actually appropriate, and also how best to organize the mediation days involved. Most independent mediation companies are willing to discuss the case with you free of charge and free of any commitment. This initial discussion will help you decide whether to go ahead with mediation, to be clear on how many days will be involved, how to set up the timings of each of the days and to specify the full costs overall.

It would be a good idea for one person in the organization to be given the overall task of organizing the team mediation and keeping everyone informed.

Checking that all formal or legal processes have been completed

If you do not make sure that all formal, legal or appeal processes associated with this team have been completed before the team mediation takes place, they could well obstruct the outcome and the success of the team mediation itself. For instance, if someone with a grievance has put in an appeal, that person could well block any movement towards agreement.

Team mediation can be offered and take place as a first stage informal resolution of an organization's personnel policy, but if there are other complaints and grievances still hanging over the team they will need to be completed or suspended in order to give the team mediation a chance.

Getting agreement from each team member

In accordance with the voluntary nature of mediation, you will need to contact each member of the team and verify their willingness and agreement to have a team mediation. If this is not given, then it is not possible for a mediation to go ahead.

In our experience, most team members do agree to mediation if it is offered to them in a positive and constructive way. Managers and team members are often relieved to hear that they will be receiving some assistance and support from their organization around what are often distressing and time-consuming interpersonal and deeply entrenched conflicts or differences.

Informing the team about mediation aims and schedule

Once it has been agreed that the mediation will go ahead, make sure you give each team member informative, clear, easy to read information about what team mediation is and what to expect (including details on the structure, the confidentiality and other ground rules and the purpose of the

Checklist for the organization of a team mediation

I Contract in two mediators who are experienced and trained in group or team workplace mediation, either from your internal mediation service (if you have one) or an independent mediation company.

I Make sure that all formal, legal or appeal processes have been completed and will not affect the outcome of the team mediation.

I If possible have one member of staff be responsible for all the organizing of the mediation.

I Give or e-mail each person in the team a mediation information pack with clearly written information as to what they can expect. This will include information about what mediation is, its structure, the ground rules of mediation and the overall purpose of the team mediation day.

I Get agreement from all team members that they are willing to participate in a team mediation, and arrange the timings and location for the one-hour 'individual meetings' with the two mediators to take place with each team member and any related management personnel appropriate to the mediation.

I Contact and support anyone returning from 'sickness leave' and ask if they have any particular 'needs' around the mediation day. Arrange additional support for them such as counselling if appropriate.

I Book a suitable venue for the team mediation day such as a training or conference centre so that staff can leave their workplace behind for one day... and give everyone directions and timings and... finally...

I *THE TEAM MEDIATION TAKES PLACE...*

team mediation day). You will usually obtain this information from your internal mediation service or from the mediation company that you contract in. It is very important to the overall success of a mediation that people know exactly what they are going to be part of and what to expect.

If this step in organizing a mediation is missed or not done well – for example the information is not clear or expressed constructively, or some people receive it and others do not – this could affect people's attitude towards the mediation and jeopardize its success right from the beginning.

Each participant in the mediation will then be given the time of his/her individual meeting with the mediators, and the date for the team mediation day. The individual meetings with each person should take place a day or two before the team mediation day or as close as possible to it. Two experienced mediators are usually required for a team mediation and both mediators need to be in on the individual meetings, so that they both hear what has been happening and they can then decide together what might be needed for the team mediation day.

Possible pitfalls in the team mediation set-up

Every group is different and not all will proceed smoothly. A few of the most frequent possible questions or 'pitfalls' are summarized below:

▌ *What to do if most of the team does not agree to mediation?* If the team overall do not agree to resolve their differences by mediation, then a mediation does not take place.

▌ *What to do if one or two people do not agree to mediation or they are absent for some reason?* It is often the case, especially in larger teams, that at least one or two people will be away on holidays or on sickness leave or sabbatical, or possibly do not agree to a mediation. It is simply a matter of making a decision to go ahead or not; it will be helpful to discuss this with your mediators.

Obviously, a team mediation should ideally include every person in the team but sometimes this is just not possible for one reason or another. Overall, if the team members who cannot attend are not crucial to the issues or conflict in the team, then it may well be that the mediation goes ahead without them. If this is the case, then you will need to think carefully about how they are informed about the mediation and to make sure they receive a copy of the mediation agreements.

▌ *What to do if someone has been off sick with stress and wants to be part of the mediation?* Naturally, a situation where someone is off sick generally, or off sick with stress or depression (possibly as a consequence of the conflict within the team), needs to be handled with great care and sensitivity.

The organization has a duty of care to make sure that a team mediation is appropriate for such people to attend. You will need to make sure that they have been signed off by their doctor as fit for work before the mediation takes place. In addition to this, you will need to speak to them about any particular needs they may have around the mediation – for instance, they may need more 'breaks' during the team mediation day or you may set up some support such as counselling sessions if you have an in-house or employee assistance scheme.

Deciding on the venue for the mediation

The individual meetings can take place in a seminar or meeting room – as long as it is private and there are no interruptions. Some organizations have suitable rooms on their own premises; others book seminar rooms in a local hotel or conference / training centre.

The team mediation day is better held in a venue that is near the workplace (so people can get to it easily) but not in it – to give people the chance to leave work behind and to participate fully in the team mediation day. So, if possible, a pleasant and conducive conference centre or hotel is a good idea for the team mediation day, and a shared lunch would add to group cohesiveness.

The structure of the team mediation day

Once all the team members have had individual meetings with the mediators, the team mediation day can then take place. For this reason a team mediation event will normally be scheduled as a two to three-day event (approximately two days for the individual meetings with the mediators and then one day for the team mediation).

The team mediation day follows the six-step structure of mediation as described in Chapter 3. It commences with chairs set in a circle so that everyone gets a chance to speak, and equality and openness are encouraged from the beginning.

The team mediation is a robust and clear process directed skilfully towards solutions, strategies and work practices that will significantly improve the way the team operates and works together. It can mean some hard work for the team to go through and openly discuss all their issues but towards the end of the day the mediators will encourage and support the group to generate and choose the solutions that will work for them. With greater numbers it may also take a longer time for all to be heard and for agreements to be reached.

As in most mediation, these solutions need to be decided upon and agreed by all team participants present and are written up at the end of the day by the mediator for everyone to sign and retain their own copy. Part of the voluntary mediation agreement also includes the date of an agreed follow-up meeting with the mediators at a convenient time in the future in order to see how the agreements are working out in practice.

The end point of a team mediation is often one of relief and renewed optimism for the team as a whole and for the team manager.

Chapter 6: The essentials

In this chapter we have examined some of the causes of team dysfunction and why team conflicts arise. We also viewed some of the possible scenarios of team breakdown that mediators may encounter and when it is most appropriate to use team mediation and when not.

We have looked at and detailed the stages you need to go through to set up and organize a team mediation, and how the six-step mediation model can be used for a larger number of people. A team or group mediation requires two mediators who have a high level of training and experience.

Team dysfunction can cause havoc with team morale and productivity. A well-planned and structured team mediation can give people the chance to deal with the real underlying issues and to change things for the better for the whole team.

7

Team mediation and group dynamics

We have looked at the nature and delivery of team mediation. In this chapter we shall examine some of the dynamics involved in working with teams and consider some of the special situations that arise and the particular skills that the mediator requires when working with groups of people.

LOOKING AT GROUP DYNAMICS

Although mediators do not need to be trained group workers to conduct team mediations, it is useful to understand something of group dynamics and the background to the evolution of group work. We shall briefly refer to books that those interested may wish to explore further (listed in the resources bibliography) and we shall view in some detail one useful general model of group dynamics that can assist mediators and managers in working with groups.

Developments in group theory and group working practice have been extensive over the last half-century. Early work deriving from social psychology conducted at Bethel, Maine, generated the group theory and methodology usually referred to as the T-Group. T-groups are analytic, behaviourally focused and concerned with group dynamics and behaviours that evolve naturally in the group and from which the group learns with the assistance and interpretation of the trainer.

Within 'person-centred therapy' and the 'counselling' movement the group was employed as a tool for interpersonal learning and self-discovery with the support of 'non-directive facilitators' as described in *Carl Rogers on Encounter Groups* (1970).

Tuckman's team-development model

One accessible model of group dynamics that is useful for team mediators can be found in the work of Dr Bruce Tuckman, who first published his model in 1965 and developed it through to his later description in 1977 (Figure 7.1). The value of this model to mediators and managers lies in helping them to recognize certain natural and predictable stages in the development of a group.

No model should ever be followed slavishly, and clearly the phases of this model may not unfold as clearly and sequentially as the description that follows. Essentially however the value of the model lies in the awareness that groups have a shared life and an overall 'growth and developmental rhythm'. Having an awareness that this unfolding and interplay in the group may, to some extent, be predictable makes the dynamic easier to recognize and to work with.

Tuckman's original model contained four 'developmental sequences' to which he gives the simple and memorable titles:

1. Forming.
2. Storming.
3. Norming.
4. Performing.

These stages are described in some detail below.

Stage 1: Forming

In the Forming stage, interpersonal relations are characterized by dependence. Group members rely on safe, patterned behaviour and look to the group leader/manager for guidance and direction. Group members have a desire for acceptance by the group and a need to know that the group is safe. They set about gathering impressions and data about the similarities and differences among them and form preferences for future sub-

```
5 STAGES OF GROUP DEVELOPMENT
```

FORMING

■ **passive, wait and see**
   follow direction from the leader/manager
   'checking out' the environment and others
   difficult topics or emotions avoided
   task oriented

STORMING

■ **competition, conflict, chaos**
   personal hostilities, power struggles
   complaints and counter complaints
   discomfort and tension in group
   absences or more time off with stress
   some people may leave

NORMING

■ **working together and group cohesion**
   relief that 'storming' stage is over
   easy cooperative working relations
   openness and sharing
   possible resistance to any change

PERFORMING

■ **interdependence**
   flexible, problem-solving
   creative and highly productive
   unity – group identity is complete, group morale is
      high, and strong group loyalty
   not reached by all groups

ADJOURNING

■ **break-up or end of the group**
   process of goodbye and the ending needs to be
   acknowledged and honoured

Figure 7.1 Team group dynamics
© Adapted from B Tuckman, 'Developmental sequence in small groups' (1965)

grouping. Rules of behaviour seem to be 'to keep things simple and to avoid controversy'. Contentious topics and feelings are therefore usually avoided at this stage.

The major task in this phase concerns *orientation*. Members attempt to orientate to the task as well as to one another. Discussion centres on defining the scope of the task, how to approach it and similar concerns. To grow from this stage to the next takes some trust in order for each member to relinquish the comfort of non-threatening topics and risk the possibility of conflict.

Stage 2: Storming

The next stage, which Tuckman calls Storming, is characterized by competition and conflict in the personal-relations dimension and in the task-functions dimension. As the group members attempt to organize for the task, conflict inevitably results in their personal relations. Individuals have to bend and mould their feelings, ideas, attitudes and beliefs to suit the group organization. Because of 'fear of exposure' or 'fear of failure', there will be an increased desire for structural clarification and commitment. Although conflicts may or may not surface as group issues, they do exist.

Questions will arise about who is going to be responsible for what, what the rules are, what the reward system is, and what the criteria for evaluation are. This stage includes conflicts over leadership, structure, power and authority. There may be wide swings in members' behaviour due to emerging competition and hostilities. Because of the discomfort generated during this stage, some members may leave and some remain completely silent, while others may attempt to push their views forward. If the underlying issues and problems are not dealt with, then they will tend to re-occur again and again in one form or another.

In order to progress to the next stage, group members must move from a 'testing and proving' mentality to a 'problem-solving' mentality. The most important trait in helping groups to move on to the next stage seems to be the ability to listen to each other's needs.

Stage 3: Norming

In Tuckman's Norming stage, interpersonal relations are characterized by cohesion. Group members are engaged in active acknowledgement of all members' contributions, community building and maintenance, and the solving of group issues. Members are willing to change their preconceived ideas or opinions on the basis of facts presented by other members, and they actively ask questions of one another. Leadership is shared and cliques dissolve. When members begin to know and identify with one another, the level of trust in their personal relations contributes to the development of group cohesion. It is during this stage of development (assuming the group gets this far) that people begin to experience a sense of group belonging and a feeling of relief as a result of resolving interpersonal conflicts.

The major task function of Stage 3 is the data flow among group members. They share feelings and ideas, solicit and give feedback to one another, and explore actions related to the task. Creativity is high. If this stage of data flow and cohesion is attained by the group members, their interactions are characterized by openness and sharing of information on both a personal and task level. They feel good about being part of an effective group.

The major drawback of the Norming stage is that members may begin to fear the inevitable future break-up of the group; they may consequently resist change.

Stage 4: Performing

The Performing stage is not reached by all groups. If group members are able to evolve to Stage 4, their capacity, range and depth of personal relations expand to true interdependence. In this stage, people can work independently, in sub-groups, or as a total unit with equal facility. Their roles and authorities dynamically adjust to the changing needs of the group and individuals. Stage 4 is marked by interdependence in personal relations and by problem solving in the realm of task functions. By now, the group should be at its most productive.

At this stage individual members have become self-reassuring, and the need for group approval is past. Members are both highly task oriented and highly people oriented. There is unity: group identity is complete, group morale is high, and group loyalty is intense. The task function becomes genuine problem solving, leading toward optimal solutions and optimum group development. There is support for experimentation in solving problems and an emphasis on achievement. The overall goal is productivity through problem solving and work.

Around 1975 Tuckman refined his original model to add a final stage that he called 'Adjourning', sometimes also referred to as 'De-forming and mourning'. Basically this stage may be described as follows.

Stage 5: Adjourning

Adjourning – the ending of a group – involves the termination of task behaviours and the disengagement from relationships. A planned conclusion usually includes recognition for participation and achievement and an opportunity for members to say personal goodbyes. Concluding a group can create some apprehension – in effect, a minor crisis. The termination of the group is a regressive movement of giving up control and inclusion in the group. The most effective interventions in this stage are those that facilitate task termination and communication to help acknowledge and process the group's 'goodbyes' and disengagement.

Clearly the mediator or manager who is able to identify, and feel comfortable with, the developmental stages exhibited by the group will be in a far better position to facilitate and to intervene appropriately. That being said, the six-step model is also a safe guiding structure that helps blend the needs of the mediation process with what can be expected of group dynamics and the sequential development contained in Tuckman's model.

MEDIATION AND SUB-PERSONALITIES

While Tuckman's model helps mediators to be aware of the likely sequential stages of group development, the model of sub-personalities, discussed below, helps mediators raise awareness of both their own inner processes and of the characteristics or roles that individuals may assume or display when in a group or team situation. John Rowan (1993) defines sub-personalities as 'permanent or semi-permanent autonomous regions of the personality'.

The concept of there being different personalities or different patterns of behaviour within one person, the concept that most refer to as 'sub-personalities', is recognized by most forms of modern psychology, including Freud (Ego, Id and Superego), Jung (Archetypes and the Shadow), Transactional Analysis (Adult, Parent, Child), Psychosynthesis (Inner Child, Inner Wise person...), Voice Dialogue (the Controller/Protector, the Inner Critic etc) and Gestalt (Top dog/Underdog).

Our personality is fundamentally a system of energy patterns that helps protect our vulnerability and we may have different parts of ourselves that want different things. When you are undecided about something, for example, one part of you might want to do one thing and another part of you wants to do something else. These can be referred to as your sub-personalities, those different parts of you that come out in your life at different times. We are not just one bland personality, inside we can be seen to have a whole variety of 'parts of ourselves' that are more complex and varied.

This model is included not for purposes of 'labelling' but rather to suggest that mediators may do well to spot these sub-personality dynamics as latent or at work both within themselves and in the mediation group. The concept of sub-personalities provides an interesting and imaginative way in which to become self-reflective while facilitating the mediation process. It also helps us spot the externalization of these inner dynamics by individual members into the general dynamic and sequences of group development.

Using this concept of different parts within us, we have created some interesting descriptions of sub-personalities that you might recognize in yourself or in others in your team.

The 'Exploder'

The Exploder is the part of you that just wants to let it all out, to explode with anger. This is the part that wants to shout back no matter the consequence. It has a strong energy of frustration about it that is hard to control. The exploder is unpredictable, can 'blow up' at any time and can be quite frightening to those around.

The 'Stirrer'

The Stirrer is the part of you that makes you want to mischievously 'stir' others around you, to incite conflicts and disagreements between other people, to make things worse in the office or in your team. It knowingly creates or joins in gossip about other work colleagues and gets a buzz from the reactions and negativity it can evoke. The stirrer often keeps in the background, inflaming other people without being noticed. Stirrers get their inner satisfaction from being able to affect others whilst not being seen as the instigators themselves. This is the part of us that wants to get at other people just for the sake of it, through boredom, lack of personal achievement or just plain bad humour.

The 'Moaner'

The Moaner is the part of you that just wants a good moan about everything or anything and is fed up with being understanding or reasonable. It will begin to moan about all the negatives in a work situation and once it gets going, does not want to stop but digs itself more and more into a pit of self-righteous grumbles and complaints. The moaner is not interested in solutions or rational ways forward because it enjoys moaning too much.

The 'Pleaser'

The Pleaser is the part of you that just wants everyone to get along and be nice to each other. It will try very hard to smooth things over, smooth other people's hurt feelings or negativity, in order to maintain a happy atmosphere at work. The pleaser is everyone's friend. It is the part of you that will say 'yes' to whatever is asked for – and will hold back your true opinions in order to keep the peace.

The 'Hurt Child'

The Hurt Child is like a little boy or girl inside you that feels hurt and 'hard done by' and wants to show it by crying or making a noise about something, by storming out, by being terribly unreasonable just for the sake of it, or by being 'victim-like' and wanting someone else to make it all OK for you. The hurt child in you can cut deep, in the sense that present day conflicts can feel a lot worse than they are because they 're-stimulate' hurts from your past.

The 'Avoider'

The Avoider is the part that just wants to 'lay low' and 'keep your head down', and hopes that things will just pass over and not affect you. This is the part of you that just wants to get on with your work and wants to avoid overly emotional or difficult people or problems. The keep-quiet part will 'avoid' as much as possible and can get quite annoyed if asked to participate or do something about the problem.

The 'Warrior or Leader'

The Warrior part of you is the part of you that is courageous and competent, willing to support and lead other people and to find ways forward in a sensible, rational and fair way. This will be the part of you that would be interested in new concepts and is willing to take risks. The warrior is often in a leadership position but not necessarily so. This part is about that aspect of you that can feel compassionate, kind, willing to 'let things go', able to take self-responsibility and see the wider perspective.

Disowned selves

This refers to those parts of ourselves that we disown or do not associate or identify with. For instance, we can identify so strongly with one part of us, say the Pleaser, that we completely dis-identify with the Exploder or angry part of us. Committed Pleasers may find it very hard to find or allow that part of themselves that can get angry or cause a commotion, particularly in a work situation.

Disowned selves can play a part in workplace conflicts because if someone disowns a particular part of themselves – in this example, the angry or explosive part – then it can mean that this person will find it very difficult to accept or deal with an Exploder when faced with one in a work or life situation. The Pleaser who cannot identify with his/her angry part will very likely be very fearful of Exploders or 'judge' them very harshly, and this could well result in interpersonal clashes and complaints.

Another example is the Warrior not identifying with their Hurt Child. This could mean that the Warrior might find it very hard to have much sympathy with the vulnerable Hurt-Child kind of person in the office and not understand why such people feel as they do. Warriors may feel quite impatient and exasperated and may even come across as unfeeling or abrupt in their unsympathetic response.

'Deep democracy'

The point of this model is that the more you are aware of all the parts of your personality, the more able you will be to encompass and understand other people and not get 'locked' into polarities with them or have to play out unhelpful or unrewarding dramas. This is what Arnold Mindell terms 'Deep democracy'. Deep democracy represents the awareness and the ability to accept 'the good, the bad and the ugly' within yourself and thereby to become able to accept it in others around you.

This theory of deep democracy also has a lot to do with truly accepting the diversity of all those personalities and people that you may come across, and as such has much meaning in the context both of mediation in general and of mediating with workplace teams and groups. It reinforces the notion that every person in a team, no matter how different from the others, brings different qualities to that team.

DEALING WITH CULTURAL DIFFERENCES: PREJUDICES, ASSUMPTIONS AND DISCRIMINATION

Another dynamic at work in any group dimension arises from the differences that proceed from culture, prejudice, assumptions or stereotyping – all things that can lead to discrimination, marginalization or even victimization and that increase or complicate what divides.

Discrimination is a very large subject in itself and so we are only able to include a few pointers here as to how such social and cultural divisions arise. We shall then list some ways in which mediators can help counteract, confront or manage any active discrimination.

The essence of discrimination is that it is a prejudice in action. A working definition of prejudice is: 'a feeling or attitude about an individual or group based on partial knowledge'. Discrimination is acting consciously or unconsciously on a prejudice and is at its most negative when our action is against someone else's interests.

The origins of discrimination: 'differences that threaten'

We are well aware in the contemporary climate of the 'group differences' that can ignite into conflict between ethnic, national, gender, class or other social or moral groupings. Conflict is often actually headlined and defined in terms of inter-cultural or inter-group differences – as if it is these differences that actually cause the conflict. In fact this is a misnomer and it is, as we have already seen, not actual 'differences' but the perception of these differences as involving a real or imagined threat to another group or culture that underlies and provokes the conflict. Tajfel and Turner (1979) suggest that the more there is conflict between groups, the more likely it will be that those individuals are judging one another on their group affiliation rather than on individual characteristics.

Prejudice and stereotyping

There is extensive academic work on the process of learned difference, of stereotyping and of prejudice (Allport, 1954; Billig, 1976; Doise, 1978). Basically such work describes how we all learn to define ourselves in a process of 'social categorization' that begins from our earliest years with our first family and social experiences. Once we have learned 'who we are' from those around us, this is reinforced by the everyday communications of our peer group. This conditioning in turn tends to reduce to a shorthand of stereotypes backed by a further shorthand of associated threats implied by these differences. In this way a set of stereotypes and scripts emerge that can easily furnish the assumptions and language of lasting 'inter-group ideologies' and their resulting conflicts.

A stereotype contains simplified judgements about a group of people that leads us to see all members of that group as having certain (usually negative) traits.

Racial and cultural diversity

Clearly cultural and racial characteristics can themselves become sources of conflict, provoking differences that often lie outside of the awareness of both parties. Studies of cultural and racial attitudes to conflict and its resolution offer very interesting insights that are of possible relevance to mediators dealing with disputants from mixed races. It appears that Asian attitudes towards society and social structures, such as those in China or Japan, incline them to what Kozan termed a _harmony_ model. In this model the individual is less significant than the group and differences tend to be played down or positions not asserted – so as to preserve social cohesion and the deference that holds families, society and organizations together. In actual conflict then, this group tends to seek third-party intervention to reduce tension and to restore harmony and group norms. By contrast in the United States, the UK and other English-speaking cultures, _individual value and personal interests_ are held to be more central in an 'egalitarian' way. This in turn leads to a more _confrontational_ social and procedural model of operating, and of business, involving the active clash of competing interests – in a way that, to certain other cultures, may appear both 'selfish' and aggressive. Finally, the Continental model, reflected in such countries as France and Spain and linked with prior colonial cultures such as South America, reflects strong social and political codes. The resulting models are more _regulative_, and references to authority, law and social codes or concordats strongly affect the group and the social response to conflict. These cultures tend, as a result, to solve conflict by arbitration, regulation or by reference to the judiciary.

Social, ethnic, cultural and stereotypical differences, then, are likely to be present in any group and can be expected to surface in team and group mediations – with potentially damaging effects on the resolution of conflict. So what is it that a mediator can do to counteract this tendency to cross cultural or inter-group division and to confront or manage prejudice as it emerges?

How to reduce prejudice and actively prevent discrimination within mediation

There are a number of ways in which the mediator can, on the one hand, model the acceptance of diversity and, on the other, confront prejudice and stereotyping. These include:

▎ *Respect*. By offering each individual non-judgemental listening and by hearing and summarizing people's expression of issues, needs and wishes, the mediator demonstrates powerfully the desired impartiality, equality and welcoming of difference and diversity.
▎ *Equality*. By ensuring that equal time, attention, consideration and conditions are offered to each and every member of the mediation, the mediator again normalizes and encourages these values.
▎ *Positive validation*. By welcoming, thanking, encouraging and praising participants as they identify their issues and differences, the mediator makes it clear that they *welcome difference* with a view to *enrichment and potential creativity* rather than as a source of division.
▎ *Ground rules*. By establishing and maintaining clear mediation ground rules on respectful communication, the mediator can challenge and even, 'if push come to shove', directly prohibit aggressive, discriminatory or abusive contributions and so reaffirm equality and respect within the mediation meeting itself.
▎ *Verbal challenge*. The essence of the language of prejudice and stereotyping is that it is *generalized* and contains large *unqualified assumptions*. This makes it possible for the mediator to verbally challenge by focusing on specifics and by clarification.

MEDIATION AND GROUP SCAPEGOATING

One of the biggest dangers in carrying out a team mediation is that the group will 'scapegoat' one particular person or persons within the team. So it is very important to have some understanding of how this may operate and to know how to avoid it happening within a mediation process.

Anti-discrimination practice for mediators

Be aware of your own prejudice or bias: mediators need to:

■ acknowledge and understand their own biases or prejudices, for or against;

■ be aware of how these may affect their behaviour or interactions with others;

■ be open and honest about what they do not understand;

■ keep informed about cultural differences;

■ maintain their professional impartiality and not give their own opinions or feelings;

■ recognize and respect differences;

■ ensure adequate support and mediation supervision.

Act in an impartial and fair way to all: mediators should ensure that they:

■ are committed to finding out what is going on from the perspectives of all parties;

■ ask fair and sensitive questions on the issues that are important to the parties;

■ avoid making judgements about people on the basis of how they express their feelings or distress, or how they communicate;

■ do not collude with the prejudice of one party towards another.

Use mediation skills to counter any bias: the mediator should:

■ give equal attention and credence to the issues, feelings and opinions of each person;

■ use appropriate and neutral language;

■ seek guidance from the parties on what appear to be culturally specific behaviours, attitudes or needs;

■ openly give reasons for decisions made within the mediation process;

■ use separate 'caucus' individual meetings with each party within the joint mediation meeting, if necessary.

Challenge and do not collude: it is within the mediator's remit to challenge discriminatory language or behaviour by:

■ challenging, or asking to cease, any discriminatory remarks or behaviours – eg, sexist, racist, disabalist – in an assertive and calm way;

■ reminding parties of the mediation ground rule of 'treating each other in a respectful manner'.

What is group scapegoating?

Scapegoating is a very harmful and negative group behaviour whereby the group or certain members of the group collude to discredit and blame a target person or sub group of people.

It is imperative that the team mediation is not seen by some members of the team as their chance to go in for the attack against someone else – whether it be a colleague or their manager. In his book *The Manufacture of Madness* (1997), Thomas Szasz writes: 'The tendency to sacrifice a scapegoat in order to save the group from disintegration... is clearly basic to man's social nature.' In other words, groups have a natural tendency to want to blame someone for their tension and difficulties, and they can be highly persistent and blind as to whom they choose to direct their hostilities towards. The person or persons they scapegoat may or may not have anything to do with the problems or dysfunctions the team are experiencing.

Often groups chose to target those who are most different from themselves. Thus, it may be possible to see scapegoating as a group's struggle to manage or deal with differences that they do not understand. It is most evident where group members are relating to each other primarily out of stereotypic or superficial judgements or biases based on such things as race, colour, gender, disability, religion, football team, class, accent, dress, ability to speak English, whether the person acts in an accepted 'polite' manner and so on.

Work teams that have been together over a long period of time will have more of a tendency to operate as 'group mind' and to ostracize those who they feel do not belong to their group. This does not bode well for those people who are new to the team or who are very different from the rest of the team, either culturally or in language or work/management style.

Often groups will attack someone who dares to think or act differently from them. The kind of subtle but highly damaging and distressing consequences of this kind of team behaviour can result in individuals feeling put down, ostracized and bullied. Sometimes the scapegoating is so indirect that it is hard for someone to articulate just what kind of bullying they are experiencing or to show hard evidence of this.

Individuals can experience scapegoating from other team members in a number of ways:

- being criticized and put down;
- being left out of chats and conversations, being cold-shouldered;
- being left out of social events outside of work;

▌ having particular needs or requests disregarded;

▌ experiencing a lack of appreciation;

▌ being the target for jokes;

▌ having suggestions or new ideas disregarded or discredited;

▌ being subject of gossip;

▌ not being given access to information;

▌ e-mails or phone calls not being returned.

How to avoid scapegoating in a team mediation

In setting up a team mediation, it is important that one person is not put in the position of having to face a number of team-mates 'having a go' at him or her. This is not the fair and equal approach that mediation needs to be.

If there are multiple and shared issues within the team, then team mediation makes sense. If it is a situation whereby most of the team are strongly against one person (whether this person is a colleague or their manager) then the mediator will need to think of creative ways of mediating between all involved in the fairest possible manner.

This may indicate that a number of one-to-one mediations rather than a whole team mediation is required in the first instance. It may be that, once these one-to-one mediations have been successful, the resultant change in attitude could mean that a whole team mediation becomes a viable and positive way forward.

In terms of the team mediation itself, it is the mediators' responsibility to ensure that: each person receives an equal amount of time; everyone's issues are elicited, and there is a controlled discussion of each of the issues; direct or indirect attacks are challenged (mainly by use of the mediation ground rules); constructive emotional communication is made possible and misassumptions are identified. The mediators will need to be creative in facilitating difficult exchanges so that they are helpful and fair to all parties.

TEAM MEDIATION AND 'GHOST FIGURES'

One of the unique aspects that can arise within group dynamics is the situation whereby someone is 'not present' and yet still exerts a significant influence on the group itself. The use of the term 'ghost role' was first developed by Dr Arnold Mindell, a Jungian analyst who went on to create a psychotherapy called Process Work, now based in the United States. 'Process Orientated Psychology', founded by Arnold and Amy Mindell (1995), has also been extensively employed in large group conflict resolution.

In the present context of mediation we are employing the term 'ghost figures' to indicate those people who were part of the team in the past or who are not part of the team now but do exert an indirect influence upon it. Such ghost figures who may not be physically present at the team mediation day may include:

- a previous manager that the team were very positively attached to;
- a previous manager or colleague that the team still have strong negative feelings about;
- a more senior manager who is part of the hierarchy of line management but does not choose to be part of the mediation;
- a team colleague who is absent due to illness, holidays or sabbatical;
- a manager or member of the team who just did not turn up on the team mediation day or suddenly phones in sick the morning of the mediation.

You may know that a ghost figure is present in the mediation when team members talk about this person a lot or certain issues keep going back to this one person; or when issues cannot be fully resolved because this particular person is not there; or when there are strong feelings coming up in the group that have something to do with this person and not so much to do with the people present.

Now, as we have said earlier, every attempt is made to get everyone in the team together for the team mediation day, but these ghost figures could be people who have left the team, left the organization altogether or gone to other parts of the organization. And even though they have left, the issues of the team can still be 'entangled' with them in some way. This makes it more difficult to mediate. If someone is not there at the mediation, then there is no prospect of resolving issues with that person. That is why they are called ghost figures; it is as if they are not there and yet they have some kind of presence, some kind of energetic influence on the group, its feelings and its dynamics.

It is important to give some recognition to this figure, this person, say his or her name, bring it out into the open, and facilitate the discussion and expression of feelings that needs to take place. This ghost figure needs to be brought into consciousness by helping the group realize what this influence is about, give them the chance to talk about it so they become free of this person's influence, free to make new choices for the team members who are present.

Some suggestions, as a team mediator, on what to do if it seems that there is a 'ghost figure' present:

▌ Bring this figure into people's awareness, name the person.
▌ Allow the group to talk about the person and what they feel about him or her.
▌ Sensitively help the group understand and recognize what effect this person has or had on the group by asking open questions.
▌ When the effect of this figure is more openly understood, bring the discussion back to the purpose of the present mediation; do not let the group get lost or too caught up with this figure.
▌ Help the group make new choices for themselves, help them make decisions about what to do with the issues facing them in present time and to move on.

This way of understanding the effect of 'ghost figures' on a group or work team is just one way of helping you to manage the effect of someone not actually present at the team mediation day who still has a strong influence on the group.

Chapter 7: The essentials

For mediators working with workplace teams there are clearly dynamics that apply to people in groups that add new dimensions to a mediation and that require a particular awareness on the part of the mediators.

Works on group dynamics and 'systems theory' are numerous and we suggest that having some wider understanding of these areas may help mediators to assess, to be aware of, and to allow for deeper aspects of the group or system with which they are working. For instance, we describe in this chapter the 'group development stages' model of Bruce Tuckman.

Other special aspects or concerns relating to group or team mediations that we cover in this chapter include: sub-personalities and deep democracy, assessing and dealing with 'cultural differences' in groups and how to handle the issues of 'scapegoating' and the effects of 'ghost figures', a term which refers to people who are absent or have left the group but who are still entangled in the consciousness of the group and are affecting team members.

8
Introducing mediation into your workplace:
mediation providers, personnel policies and mediation practice in the organization

It is clear that the UK government, like that in many other countries, is now encouraging organizations to use some form of dispute resolution to attempt to resolve grievances well before they escalate into formal or legal complaints.

The majority of organizations are opting for mediation as their preferred dispute resolution method. This support of mediation and alternate dispute resolution procedures is mainly based on a wish to reduce the number of formal complaints ending up at employment tribunals and to encourage more positive and effective communication and 'dialogue' within the workplace itself.

The UK Employment Act 2002 – Dispute Resolution Regulations, which came into force in October 2004, backed this up by effectively penalizing both employees and employers if they do not 'exhaust internal dispute resolution strategies' as a first step. The subsequent review by Gibbons in his 2007 report recommends that organizations use and support mediation as early on in a dispute as possible in order to reduce disruption to both the workplace and the individuals involved.

Introducing mediation into your workplace – so it is integrated into the fabric of the work culture and into your policies – takes careful thought and planning. The uptake of mediation by staff, its success rate and its long-term future depends on how it is established and upon your prior thinking around some of the key questions that we shall set out to address in this chapter, summarized in the box below.

Some key questions

- Who is going to do the mediation?
- Will you use internal or external mediators?
- Where do you find external mediators?
- How do you select internal mediators from your staff?
- What training will these internal mediators need?
- What support and supervision will you give to your mediators?
- How will your internal mediation service operate?
- How will mediation be part of your personnel polices?
- How will you disseminate mediation throughout your organization so everyone knows about it?

WHO IS GOING TO CARRY OUT THE MEDIATIONS?

The choices that you have, in terms of who is going to carry out workplace mediation, are: external mediators, internal mediators or a combination of both. How you make this decision will depend on such factors as:

- Do you want mediation to be very much a part of your organization and fully integrated, or do you only want it to be a small sideline with minimum use? If you want it to be taken on board by employees, to be part of a work culture of creative conflict resolution and problem solving, and for all your employees to have access to it, then it would be well worth your while thinking about creating your own internal mediation service within your organization.

  If it is only going to be used occasionally, then calling in experienced external mediators may be the most cost-effective and appropriate approach.

  A conflict audit and cost comparisons may need to be made.
- How many issues, such as grievance or bullying complaints, does your organization have to deal with in a year?

The more complaints and potential conflicts you have, the more it makes sense to have your own mediators. If you have only a few cases a year, then external mediation could well be the best option.

▌ How important is the 'independence' of the mediator?

The beauty of mediation is that the mediator is independent, does not have a personal 'agenda' and will be impartial and skilled enough to facilitate a successful mediation even with the most complex of cases. It is very important to the success of mediation that the parties view or perceive the mediator as someone who does not take sides and who is able to treat everyone with equality and fairness.

Some organizations have decided that their staff might see internal mediators as being too much 'on the side of the organization' and have made the decision to call in or to set up a 'retention contract' with an external mediation consultancy. Others have gone for their own internal mediation service where this has not been a limiting or major issue.

A further combined option would be to set up an internal mediation team but to call upon external mediators where the complexity of the case or the seniority of those involved in the mediation requires the skills of an external, experienced, independent mediator.

▌ Finally, does your organization have the will and the funds to create its own internal mediation service?

It is no mean feat to set up a mediation service from scratch, and to do this you will need the full backing of policy makers/senior management or directors in your organization as well as the finances to match this.

Internal mediation has worked the best where it has been taken on as a whole organizational response to resolving conflicts and not just piecemeal. This means it must have the backing of those who hold the power and the necessary budget to support it.

WHERE DO YOU FIND EXTERNAL MEDIATORS?

In the absence of an overall workplace mediation professional body in the UK, most organizations find external mediators by word of mouth, by Internet search or by indirect information from relevant articles or adverts.

The authors of this book are an example of independent external mediators providing workplace mediation throughout the UK and worldwide, and there are more independent mediation companies emerging every day as mediation grows and increases in use.

Overall, providers of external mediation include independent workplace mediation companies, employment law firms, counselling at work EAP providers or conciliation services, and increasingly individual consultants or human resource individuals setting themselves up as workplace mediators.

As there are many sectors in mediation – such as community mediation, family mediation and commercial mediation – probably one of the most important and obvious factors is to find a provider who is experienced in and specializes in 'workplace mediation' in particular.

The advantages of external mediation are:

■ _Speed of setting up._ Usually mediation can be arranged within a couple of weeks of initial contact.
■ _Cost efficiency._ The majority of mediations are completed in one day (more complex conflicts or team mediations will take two or three days).
■ _Resource efficiency._ Speedy resolution saves the valuable time of your staff or management.
■ _Expertise._ External mediators are usually carrying out mediations full time, have years of experience and have a high level of skill and expertise in this specialist field.
■ _Independence._ External mediators are independent of the organization and do not know or will not be meeting the parties to the mediation in any other context. This is very important in terms of boundaries and impartiality or perceptions of impartiality as well as the confidentiality of the process.

HOW DO YOU SELECT INTERNAL MEDIATORS FROM YOUR STAFF?

Once you have decided on an internal mediation service, you will need to think about which of your staff you train to be mediators.

Most organizations have selected staff to train from:

■ human resource personnel;
■ senior managers, managers, team leaders, supervisors;
■ counselling or welfare or occupational health staff;
■ harassment officers/harassment contact advisors;

- diversity or equal opportunities officers;
- complaints staff;
- trade union representatives.

Others have selected from throughout the organization in terms of different departments, different grades and possibly from different ethnic and other groups within the organization. There is often a combination of all of the above.

In particular, many organizations have opted to give workplace mediation training to their human resource staff, which works well overall. It gives them added skills within their everyday personnel work, and they are well placed to deal with mediation cases. What is important however is that they are very clear on their boundaries. When HR staff are in the role of mediators, they need to set aside their personnel advice-giving role and make it clear to the parties that, in this circumstance, they are acting as impartial mediators. These different roles must remain distinct and very clear.

Also, it is very important that, when human resource personnel are acting as internal mediators, someone else within HR deals with any personnel aspects of the case. The mediating staff must not do both with the particular mediation case they take on. Some organizations have decided to separate their mediation service away from the human resource function and have opted to train a cross section of staff.

The advantages of internal mediation are:

- *easier access* for all employees;
- *flexibility* in terms of timing and arranging mediation meetings;
- *cost effectiveness* if there are a high number of complaints;
- *inside knowledge* of the organization and its work culture and procedures;
- *encouragement* of a 'whole' organizational response to conflict resolution;
- *promotion* of positive responses and changes in the 'work culture' to the way differences and conflicts are dealt with.

WHAT TRAINING WILL INTERNAL MEDIATORS NEED?

Those who are expected to carry out mediations for inter-employee conflicts and complaints need to receive a fully accredited training in workplace mediation. These accredited courses are offered as both public courses or as in-house trainings for staff and most training providers in the UK have courses taking around six training days in all.

Each of these UK training providers has usually selected a specific national accrediting body (ie, OCN or OCR) to accredit and validate their course. Because, as yet, there is no overall accepted UK professional or accrediting body for workplace mediation, the form of accreditation or the accreditation body selected has been up to these independent training providers.

What is most important is that your internal mediators do, in fact, receive good professional skills training as well as ongoing supervisory support. There is no set law or regulation about this in the UK, but it is obvious that if your mediators are not fully trained and do not have these specialist skills then it is very likely that the situation could be made a lot worse by their attempts to mediate.

It is important that you choose training that is geared specifically to mediation in the workplace rather than general courses in mediation skills and that is nationally accredited (some providers only give their own certificate of attendance, which is not externally validated). You will also need to work out how internal mediators are going to balance their present workload or get time off from their departments to carry out mediations.

If a case were to go on to an employment tribunal, then it is important to demonstrate that your mediators have received adequate skills training from a recognized accredited training provider.

SUPERVISION OF INTERNAL MEDIATORS

Once the staff you have selected have received accredited training, they should then be supported in their mediation work and caseload by receiving individual or group supervision by an experienced workplace mediator.

Supervision can also be arranged by telephone – particularly important when new mediators are in the middle of a complex mediation and need guidance and de-briefing. The mediation training provider you contract to train your staff can usually provide the supervision you need.

HOW WILL MEDIATION BE PART OF YOUR PERSONNEL POLICIES?

Mediation is usually written into such personnel policies as:

- grievance;
- harassment/bullying;
- equal opportunities;
- dignity at work;
- equality and diversity;
- or a stand-alone mediation policy.

Informal first stage

It is within this first informal stage of existing policies that mediation is usually offered as 'a voluntary confidential option for resolving the complaint'. The earlier the intervention, the more successful mediation will be.

Mediation is more appropriate for less serious complaints and where there may be misunderstandings on both sides. If the complaint is more serious, and certainly if it is a matter of gross misconduct or criminal behaviour, then this is clearly a disciplinary matter and not mediatable. Mediation is a highly effective dispute resolution method, but it is not a panacea for everything.

Offering mediation at this informal stage within your existing personnel policies gives people the chance to understand how their behaviour or language might be affecting another person and to change it. The communication and dialogue within a mediation meeting can help people enormously in understanding each other, and even deeply entrenched intractable personal conflicts can find resolution.

Many harassment policies, within this first stage, suggest that those who are experiencing harassment or bullying, should, in the first instance, go to the person doing this and ask them to stop, with the option of being accompanied by someone such as a colleague or a manager. This may work if the conflict is about one particular issue or incident, but if the situation is more complex then this kind of approach could well make the other person very defensive.

It would make sense that this 'meeting' and the communication and dialogue that needs to take place could be more constructive and more supportive of those involved if it was facilitated by an experienced

Workplace mediation and personnel policies

Mediation can be written into an organization's existing policies, such as:

Grievance
Harassment and bullying
Dignity at work
Equal opportunities
and others.

FIRST-STAGE INFORMAL RESOLUTION
Most workplace mediation (approximately 80 per cent) is offered within this first stage of an organization's policy – for optional confidential resolution between those involved.
This earlier stage is the best time to use mediation.

or

AFTER FORMAL INVESTIGATION
When 'no fault' or 'insufficient evidence' has been found, mediation can be offered or recommended in order to rebuild working relations, either between those directly involved or often, by this time, with other colleagues or the team. Mediation at this later stage is more difficult as feelings and positions have usually escalated but people still need to work together.

or

Some organizations have opted to write a separate

MEDIATION POLICY
In order to set out how mediation can be accessed and used appropriately by all employees and managers.

mediator. A facilitated mediation is much more likely to succeed than an ad hoc direct approach, and will also result in clear, workable changes and agreements.

As mediation is more successful the earlier it takes place, then the best time to offer it is at an early stage – before positions get too extreme and unmovable. We would estimate that 80 per cent of mediations presently take place at this informal first stage of a personnel policy. If, however, mediation proves unsuccessful, formal or legal measures can then be invoked.

Formal investigation

Sometimes complaints go directly to a formal investigation. For those cases where 'insufficient evidence' or 'no fault' has been found after an investigation has taken place, then mediation can be offered or recommended in order to facilitate the 'rebuilding of working relationships' because people still need to work together.

At this point, working relationships have often deteriorated to a very low point with a lot of strongly negative feelings and other people, such as team colleagues, may now be involved. Something needs to happen or be put in place to help people come to terms with the aftermath of the investigation and to get back to functional, respectful working relations. Mediation at this later stage is often more difficult as feelings and positions have escalated, but it can still be very helpful to move things on and can often involve both a mediation between the parties involved in the initial complaint and a team mediation.

To summarize, mediation can be used after formal or legal measures have taken place, assuming no fault has been found and the people involved are willing and still need to find a way to work together.

A mediation policy

Some organizations are choosing to introduce a new stand-alone mediation policy into their organization that outlines and details how mediation can be accessed and used appropriately. The advantage of this is that employees can request a mediation (when they are not getting on with someone) without making it into a formal grievance or harassment complaint that can have the effect of pushing people into adversarial positions even before they begin. It also means that the organization is giving its employees the clear message that it encourages constructive resolution of conflicts and differences at an early stage, before they escalate into more negative behaviours and formal or legal investigations and counter-complaints.

A mediation policy would seem to be the best practice for the introduction of mediation into a company or organization that seriously wants to 'embed' it into the work culture.

DISSEMINATION OF MEDIATION THROUGHOUT YOUR ORGANIZATION

Once you have decided to include mediation in your organization, it is vital to introduce and disseminate it so everyone knows what it is and how to best use or access it. Some actions to consider include:

- Carrying out some initial research – initiating a 'conflict audit' to see how conflicts are presently being dealt with by your organization, how people feel about the way in which conflicts and differences are handled, how much valuable management time conflicts are taking up, how many complaints are received and what kind of complaints, and so on.
- Deciding on which dispute resolution methods and strategies your organization needs.
- Deciding on whether to write mediation into existing personnel policies or to create a new mediation policy.
- Informing staff of your mediation policy and procedures (whether this relates to external mediation provision or your own internal mediation service) via staff training or induction training, staff presentations or seminars. Other forms of information or publicity could include the use of workplace mediation videos, posters, notices in staff handbooks or in pay slips or on your web site, and involvement and liaison with trade union representatives.
- Establishing some general mediation and conflict skills training for managers and staff. Alongside the accredited training in mediation, it would be enormously beneficial to cascade mediation and conflict resolution skills training throughout your organization to as many managers or team leaders as possible. The purpose of this would be to give them a basic understanding of what workplace mediation entails, when to refer disputes on to mediation, and some practical conflict management skills to resolve everyday conflicts and difficulties before they escalate. This kind of in-house training for your managers and staff would support and ensure the best use and dissemination of mediation throughout your work force, as well as giving managers the 'tools' to resolve conflicts at root level more effectively and quickly.

It goes without saying that for mediation to be introduced into an organization, it has to be planned and well thought out so that staff can see its benefits and not view it as yet another fad that management have thought up. It is our consistent experience that once staff have been introduced to what mediation is actually about, they have welcomed it with interest and enthusiasm.

Chapter 8: The essentials

Organizations are now being encouraged by the UK government and new employment law regulations to put their 'internal dispute resolution' methods clearly in place.

Most are choosing mediation provided by independent external mediators or by their own internal staff mediators, the pros and cons of which we discuss in this chapter.

Creating your own 'internal mediation service' takes planning and support in order for it to be integrated into the work culture and to become a 'whole organizational' approach and not just piecemeal. Staff who are expected to carry out workplace mediation need accredited professional skills training in this specialist subject and ongoing supervision support.

Mediation is mostly used as a first stage-option within such personnel policies as grievance, harassment and bullying, equal opportunities and dignity at work or as a stand-alone mediation policy. It can also be used after a formal investigation has taken place when no fault has been found, in order to help parties to resume functional, respectful working relations.

The sooner mediation is offered, the more likely will be its success.

PART II

Mediation in action:
case studies of real life workplace mediations

In Part II we shall deepen our understanding of the uses and workings of workplace mediation by describing a series of case studies
based upon composites of real life mediations. The names and
details in the case studies have been changed in order to preserve
confidentiality.

These examples include a variety of situations, from disputes
between employees over matters involving bullying, sexual harassment and racial issues, to conflicts within teams and between teams
and finally to conflict resolution in the boardroom.

9
Case studies of workplace mediation between two employees

We depicted early on the example of a breakdown in working relation-ships between Mark and Wendy – a typical example of the kind of conflict situation that can escalate into a bullying complaint against a manager and a counter-complaint.

In this section, we want to give you some real life case studies of how independent mediation can be carried out for a number of different types of workplace disputes. We have covered the theory; now we shall have a look at how mediation can be used in practice.

A MEDIATION FOR A COMPLAINT OF BULLYING AGAINST A MANAGER

One day, a human resources manager from a large computer software company phoned to talk about a difficult situation the HR staff were dealing with. A valued team manager called Nicola had approached her personnel department to talk about her complaints and difficulties with her line manager, John.

The HR manager described on the phone how Nicola was quite distressed about the way she felt her manager was treating her – talking to her in an abrupt manner, twice saying critical things to her in front of colleagues – and how it had all got a lot worse since a recent team meeting in which she felt he had put down one of her ideas far too harshly. Since then, she had been experiencing a lot of anxiety, not sleeping well, and was thinking of taking time off with stress.

The nub of the matter was that she felt John, her manager, did not like or support her, and since this team meeting things had deteriorated as they now both tried to avoid each other, which certainly was not helping with the project work they had to deliver and the pressured deadlines that they were now facing. They were presently at a place of only communicating the minimum to each other and, if they did speak at all, their exchange was laden with an unspoken tension. A no win situation for productivity, human or otherwise.

Nicola decided she wanted to put in a complaint through the company's bullying and harassment policy and was willing to look at what the first stage of this policy – informal resolution through mediation – could offer her. (The company had only recently written mediation into its policy.)

The HR manager explained fully what mediation was and also gave her clear written information on its structure, principles and what to expect. It was explained that mediation was a confidential and safe way for her to talk with John about their difficulties and issues together so they could find a way forward and see what was needed for things to be improved. An independent mediator would be chosen from outside of the company and be impartial and experienced in facilitating this mediation meeting between them both. Understandably, Nicola was a little wary at first and said she would think it over and let them know the next day.

The next day, she decided to go ahead with the mediation – saying that she wanted to stay in this department, that she liked her job and that she did not want this situation to get in the way or obstruct her hopes for promotion. So she was willing to undertake a mediation in order to find out if things could improve. The HR manager, now clear that Nicola was willing to engage in mediation, went to see John privately and explained the situation.

John was surprised and somewhat put out that Nicola had made this complaint. He had his own issues about Nicola but again, in brief, he said he would be willing to have a mediation meeting with her as long as it was confidential because he wanted the situation resolved as quickly as possible.

After the phone discussion, the HR manager decided to go ahead with the independent mediator and available dates were discussed. It was agreed that the mediation would take place the following week and a suitable private room in a nearby conference centre was booked by the organization.

The mediator had individual meetings lasting about one-and-a-half hours with both Nicola and John throughout the morning. From the beginning, it was clear that they had very different perspectives on what was going on. They both strongly blamed each other in different ways. The mediator mainly listened to each one and also took this opportunity to explain what mediation was about and how it could offer them a way forward if they were willing. At the end of these individual meetings with the mediator, both were in agreement with coming together in the joint face-to-face mediation that took place that afternoon.

In the first part of the mediation, John and Nicola found it very hard to talk to each other as there was a lot of resentment and blame on both sides. Nicola expressed her pent-up anger and hurt at the way she felt treated and John retaliated with his annoyance. Through persistence and the mediation process, they did manage some difficult but constructive discussion. Once everything had been expressed and the issues identified, they eventually came to the point where they had a choice, either to walk out or to start looking at each of the issues and agree the changes that were clearly needed.

This was a very delicate point in the mediation. It was either going to work and they would move forward or they would give up on each other completely. The mediator had to handle this with great sensitivity and give them the necessary space to think and to be clear that they were willing to move forwards.

Slowly but surely, they both began to look again at the issues and how they were communicating with each other. In this case, John was the first to offer a small movement forward by saying he might be willing to think again about how he gave feedback to Nicola. Nicola accepted this first 'olive branch' and then began to offer what she was willing to do differently. This was the point of change in the mediation.

From then on, the communication got easier and easier and the flow of conversation between them meant that they tackled each issue that had been identified. They worked hard at looking for a solution to each and every one of the issues that they had uncovered in the mediation. By the end of the mediation meeting, they had created seven specific mediation agreements, including the ways they were going to communicate with each other, how feedback was going to be delivered and where, how supervision meetings were going to operate, and what they were going to do if difficulties like this should arise in the future.

At the end of the mediation, they both signed and kept a copy of these agreements – which also were useful for reference when they had their follow-up meeting with the mediator three months later to see how the agreements were working out.

When the mediator did go back to see them again, things had moved on significantly; both said that they were working a lot better together since the mediation had taken place. They felt the mediation had cleared the air and helped them get on and work together in a more 'respectful' and easy way.

They were not exactly best friends, but they had managed to find a way of communicating with each other and working together in a more accepting and respectful way that both felt was an improvement on what had been happening previously.

A MEDIATION FOR A COMPLAINT OF SEXUAL HARASSMENT

Erica and Robert worked together within a team of carers for over five years. Erica complained to her personnel manager that Robert was sexually harassing her – touching her when speaking to her, occasionally putting his arm around her when in the office and asking inappropriate questions about her personal life.

When Robert was approached about all this, he claimed he had no idea what she was talking about, that they were good friends and that he was just being 'his friendly self'. He said he could not understand why Erica was complaining about him.

Of course, in cases of harassment, it is 'the perception of the person being harassed' that is important and an organization does have to take it seriously and deal with it with sensitivity.

Again in this case, mediation was written into this organization's policies as 'an optional first step for resolution' for less serious complaints of this nature. The other alternative was to set up a formal investigation. In this case, Erica did not want to go down the formal route but she did want a way of telling Robert what was upsetting her and for it to stop.

This particular mediation just took one day as there was a basic willingness to resolve on both sides. There were some long and highly sensitive and difficult discussions in this mediation meeting but with some skilful facilitating by the mediator, they came up with very clear agreements. These related to no physical touching, no inappropriate language or questions, and to Erica also agreeing to let Robert know if he was overstepping her boundaries.

Both Erica and Robert were pleased and relieved with the results of the mediation. They managed to bring about the changes that were needed in a way that felt respectful and workable and that also kept their working relationship intact.

A MEDIATION BETWEEN TWO COLLEAGUES SHARING AN OFFICE AND ALLEGED RACISM

When it comes to allegations of possible racism, there is often a huge amount of fear and anxiety surrounding the whole situation. Since the Stephen Lawrence case, many organizations are so fearful of 'getting it wrong' that managers can end up ignoring issues or side-stepping them or passing them on, often feeling that they do not have the necessary skills to deal with the situation.

There is ongoing useful debate around whether mediation is suitable for these kinds of complaints. Some feel that racism is too serious to be suitable for mediation, while others say mediation is appropriate to consider if the complaints are 'less serious' in nature and are part of a number of different issues between people.

It is difficult to say that any kind of 'racism' is 'less serious' as organizations are legally bound to take action against those who directly or indirectly discriminate on the grounds of race – and quite rightly so. There may be situations, however, where someone might feel that their conflict with a colleague, manager or team might involve elements of racism but is not sure or there have been no specific incidents or evidence of this.

This kind of situation could well benefit from the kind of communication that takes place within a mediation – where people can say what they want to say to the other and check out assumptions or ask for changes that feel more respectful to them. Mediation can give people the chance to sort these kinds of issues out between them. It keeps the communication respectful and constructive and can bring about understanding and changes that are more satisfactory for both parties. Here is an example.

Bernadette had her own office for six years. One August, while she was away on holiday, her manager had to make the decision to put someone else in her office: a female colleague, on the same grade, who was doing similar work but who had been previously working in an office on the other side of the city.

Circumstances meant that this decision had to be made hastily. Manjit and her desk and computer were moved in with the idea that she and Bernadette share both the office and the workload. When Bernadette came back and was informed of this, she was not happy, and from that moment on, she tended to ignore Manjit and also kept most of the work under her own control.

After a few weeks of this, Manjit went to her line manager to say that she was very stressed, that she thought Bernadette was not talking to her, which she thought 'might be on racist grounds', and that Bernadette went to lunch and chatted away to her other friends around the rest of the building but never invited Manjit. There was also the issue of how difficult she found it to share work with Bernadette, especially as Bernadette had been in this office for a long time and most people came to her with their queries. Her manager contacted their personnel officer about this situation, who then spoke to both Manjit and Bernadette separately.

Bernadette's side of the story (apart from her upset over how the move came about) was that she thought Manjit was very unfriendly and abrupt, that she had tried to make the situation better but it had not worked, and that she was overloaded with work and resented Manjit for not doing her fair share.

The personnel officer understood the organization's policy on race discrimination very well but he was clear that in this case, there were insufficient grounds for a formal complaint. He was also clear that it was important to take some action about this situation. From this, he decided to offer Bernadette and Manjit a mediation, to which they both agreed. If either one of them had not, then of course the mediation would not have gone ahead.

As usual in mediation, the mediator first had individual meetings with both Bernadette and Manjit, during which they spoke about what they thought was happening and expressed their feelings and reactions about this. They held different points of view of the situation – but at the same time, it was clear that it was in both their interests to find a way forward.

The afternoon face-to-face joint mediation actually went much better than they had thought it would. The individual meetings had seemed to help both of them in terms of their feelings and difficulties, so by the time we were together in the mediation meeting in the afternoon they both seemed more relaxed and more willing to talk and discuss possible solutions.

There certainly were a lot of misunderstandings and misperceptions about how they understood the situation and by talking these through over two to three hours, they eventually came to some voluntary agreements on how things could be improved in the future. These, in brief, were around communicating with each other in a respectful manner and having regular meetings on how to better distribute the workload.

At the end of the mediation, both were clearly very reassured and pleased with the outcome and went on to share the office and work in a way that made both of them much happier with their working relationship.

MOVING THROUGH THE EYE OF THE STORM AND THE ART OF THE IMPOSSIBLE: A MEDIATOR'S VIEW OF THE PROCESS

It is good to write up all these typical examples of real life workplace mediations as it gives you the details and sequence of what can happen. Here at the end of this chapter, we would like to offer you more of the flavour and the feeling of the energetic flow of the process from a more personal perspective as a mediator.

When someone phones up to discuss or request a mediation, the scenario or relationship breakdown that they describe so often sounds utterly hopeless and impossible that it is quite remarkable. As a mediator I have thought about this over the years: about how many of these situations appear 'impossible', as if there is absolutely no way out.

Many mediation scenarios are also often accompanied by a lot of unspoken anxiety as if they are permeated or surrounded by an atmosphere of fear or inevitable doom. Obviously, this reflects the conflict itself, as well as the exasperation and feelings of the HR staff or managers left to deal with such tricky and complex 'people' situations. At this point, a mediation or a workable solution for these people does feel impossible.

I have learnt from experience not to allow these feelings to affect or influence me. What sees me through is the knowledge and experience that, no matter how unfeasible a mediation may appear at the beginning, you just never know how it is going to work out in reality. You may think you do, but you don't: you just do not know. Time and time again, I have seen the most intractable situation turn into the most creative and the most graceful of successful mediations between people. I have learnt to believe in this possibility. As I say to mediation trainees, 'trust the process'. When all seems impossible, when you do not know what to do next, trust the mediation process: it will lead you through the most turbulent of storms.

Nine times out of 10, the mediation structure itself, if clearly explained and skilfully enacted, will transform the most intractable situation into something that you could not foresee. I have had situations where for instance someone is described as the most unreasonable and the most unbearable of colleagues or managers, and yet, by the end of the mediation, this person is showing such heightened awareness and willingness to improve the situation that the process ends as a great success. Parties to the mediation have so often surprised me by coming up with a whole raft of solutions and strategies and proposals to resolve a situation that first appeared so completely stuck and immovable.

So to return to the analogy of the storm – from the viewpoint of the mediator. At first, you hit the outer layer of the storm and are buffeted by the turbulence of the feelings in and around the conflict itself, which can affect everyone that comes into contact with it. Then you begin the journey of the mediation process, which takes time and concentration and patience as you navigate and move through those very difficult sticking points, hurts and recriminations where people have strong feelings and will not budge an inch. And then, after some time, something different begins to happen that is not easy to describe.

Somewhere along the line in the mediation meeting, there comes a point when things begin to change. Maybe one of the parties shows they have really understood the other; maybe one of them acknowledges that just maybe they could look at doing things differently; maybe someone offers a solution or an olive branch that just turns the whole thing around. Whatever it is, this point in the mediation is quite palpable.

It is the point of change that many mediators will recognize. It is here, at this point that I will leave some silence, some space. It is as if the world sits still for a moment: we have reached the 'eye of the storm' when after some moments, something else becomes possible, something different begins to happen. Once we have reached this point, the mediation often moves more quickly and clearly towards a whole list of agreements and solutions.

From there on, it is easy sailing and we just need to be careful to make sure we deal with all the issues that need to be dealt with in the mediation, and that in our enthusiasm we do not overlook the details and specifics of each of the mediation agreements. The parties to the mediation may not reach such a point of understanding and open communication again, so it is important that what is needed to be said is said and what is needed to be done is done – so that they can go back to everyday work life with something better, something completed.

Moving through the eye of the storm is like moving from confusion, impossibility and fear to a space of calm and often surprising resolution.
'Trust in the structure and process of mediation' is the guiding force.

Chapter 9: The essentials

Mediation can be offered for personality clashes and less serious complaints of harassment and bullying, sexual harassment, and complaints of racist or sexist behaviour.

It gives people the chance to understand why their behaviour is unacceptable and to change it.

The beauty of mediation is that people often only really 'hear' or understand what has been happening for the other person when they have their face-to-face joint mediation meeting.

These meetings of minds, emotions and interests can sometimes be dramatically transformative but are sometimes more pedestrian. What counts in the end is the degree to which the agreements reached can provide new ground to heal rifts and to help establish and build new and positive behaviours and better experiences for the future.

If people are interested in finding solutions and want to explore ways of improving how they work together, then mediation is the most positive way forward and can help even with the most intractable of situations.

10
Case studies of workplace mediation with teams

In this chapter we shall present examples of team mediations in action. We have chosen two cases, with a view to giving examples of handling different sizes of group and a range of complex issues faced by the mediators.

As with our previous case studies all the following accounts of team mediation are included to illustrate typical issues and situations and are based loosely on real or composite situations. However for the sake of preserving the confidentiality and privacy of those involved, the context, the circumstances and the exact content of the examples, have been changed.

TEAM CASE STUDY ONE: A TEAM WITH MULTIPLE PROBLEMS

Type of organization. A large charity providing vocational and employment training to 16–20-year-olds.

Number of people in the team. 12 in total: seven men and five women, from a range of different cultural backgrounds.

Complaints

1. The new manager has complained that she is being bullied by three males in the team.
2. An informal complaint of racism has been made by two women against another male team member who they say engages in 'white male banter' in front of them.
3. The most recent complaint is about two women who had a shouting match in the office and have both submitted grievance complaints against each other.

The situation

The 12 people in this team were experiencing multiple layers of difficulty and dysfunction that had been going on for a long time. Their previous manager had resigned eight months earlier because of a conflict within the team over moving offices. The team had put in a formal grievance complaint against the manager for not consulting them adequately about this move. There was also one incidence at the time of verbal aggression from one team member against the manager, who went off on stress sickness after this incidence and later resigned without returning to work.

This past history was still affecting both the team and the new manager, who came into post just two months ago. The team were still feeling aggrieved and mistrusting of management, and the new manager felt anxiety about managing this team.

After only two months in post, the manager went to her HR officer to complain about three male members of the team who she felt were not accepting her decisions and were undermining her authority and bullying her. She did not have concrete evidence of this as such, but explained that that was how she felt and it was more their attitude to her that she did not like. When the HR officer spoke to the men concerned, they denied it outright and expressed anger at their manager for 'making up complaints' against them.

In the midst of dealing with this complaint, two other grievances came into HR from two female members of this team who had had a 'shouting match' in the office (totally unrelated to the manager and her complaints). Each submitted complaints against the other.

Overall, it was clear that both the manager and the team were in trouble. There was a negativity and lethargy throughout the team. The team meetings were not working well at all and there was a general atmosphere of non-cooperation and resentment. Office space was not ideal, there was a basic lack of space and facilities, and at the same time the workload was increasing.

Something had to be done, both for the team and their manager but crucially also for the young people they were training. Their work was highly valuable in helping young people receive skills training that would help them obtain employment. It does not take a genius to recognize that the quality of their work had become poorer and poorer over the last two years despite the increase in demand. The team was obviously not working well and there was a real danger that if this situation remained unmanaged, a more serious incident or more serious complaints would arise.

The HR director, after discussions with the chief executive of the charity and the manager of the team, decided to go down the route of mediation. They decided to offer the team and its manager a team mediation to be carried out by independent workplace mediation consultants. At the next team meeting, the HR manager explained the support they wanted to give the team in the form of a team mediation and answered any questions or concerns.

Each person was also given a comprehensive 'mediation pack' to inform them of what it was all about. At the following team meeting a week later, the HR officer checked that everyone was willing to be part of the mediation and arranged the timings for the individual meetings with the mediators and the team mediation day.

This team all agreed to the mediation (apart from one person who was on secondment and would not be back for another five months) mainly because they had had enough and wanted something to be done. They wanted some help and support with the disarray they found themselves in and welcomed some external input in order for things to change.

The team mediation

Individual meetings

The team mediation began with two experienced workplace mediators having individual meetings with each member of the team, including the manager, over a period of two days. Because of the number of people involved and the long history of difficulties, many different issues and concerns were voiced, including some allegations of possible racism within the team ('white male banter' as two females put it and also one African-Caribbean man feeling somewhat left out by others in the team), the new manager feeling 'undermined', several in the team feeling 'unsupported' by their manager, two men who had had a shouting match

over work practices, new projects being unsupported, a lack of cooperation and a high level of sickness absence in the team overall.

The team mediation day

Straight after the individual meetings with all the team members and the
manager, the mediators facilitated the team mediation day, which took
place at a large conference centre in the countryside not far from the work
premises. A large room was set up with a circle of chairs and there were
two break-out rooms in case they were needed. Everyone had agreed to
the timings of the day, 9.30 in the morning to 5.30 in the afternoon, with a
shared lunch together.

Despite the difficult beginnings and the complexity and intensity of the
issues involved, the day went remarkably well. The process and structure
of team mediation have been described in Chapter 6, but essentially this
was the basic sequence of this mediation:

- Agreement to the mediation ground rules was confirmed, as was the
participants' willingness to resolve their situation through mediation.
All members were initially given an equal chance to say what they
thought had been happening in the team working relations and to
outline the issues as they saw them.
- The mediators wrote the main issues up on a flipchart and checked
with the team if they wanted to add any more that they wanted to
discuss in the mediation.
- Each issue was discussed one by one, both by open group discussion
and also later on by splitting into four sub-groups for discussion.
- The team were asked to offer solutions for each of the issues and these
were discussed until the whole team felt happy and satisfied with the
agreements they came to.
- At the end of the day these mediation agreements were typed up by the
mediators, signed by all present and each person was given a copy.

In this particular mediation, the mediators also decided to include some
positive group work around each team member sharing what they liked
about their work, what had inspired them to do it, what they wanted from
their team and what they appreciated about each other. This kind of affir-
mative and deeper level work with the group alongside the clear structure
of the mediation meant that something really changed in this team. At the
end of the day, there was a very special sense of increased confidence,
many smiles and a renewed optimism together.

This, in fact, was a turning point. The team went on to work far better
together and with a lot more mutual appreciation and support.

It was agreed by all concerned that the mediation had resolved the outstanding grievance complaints. To this point in time, no further complaints have been submitted. The new manager is still managing and has since used a more assertive management leadership style, which seems to be working. She is also supporting herself by having individual coaching sessions.

The charity has recently been awarded more funds and has already begun to plan an extension to its training premises. The team still have differences now and again, of course, but overall are managing to work well together, and since the mediation three new people have joined them.

TEAM CASE STUDY TWO: A MEDIATION BETWEEN SENIOR MANAGERS AND TWO TEAMS

Type of organization. A large PR and publishing concern located in South-East England.

Number of people in the team. Three managers, and two teams with a total of 16 members. The inter-team situation in question was between the Internal Services and Customer Services teams and the conflict also included the management team of three senior managers. The Internal Services team comprised five women and two men, and the Customer Services team comprised six women and three men. Each team had a team leader and a services section manager led the two teams; all three managers were male.

Complaints

1. The two team leaders had got into a deadlock but had not as yet formalized their grievances. Their teams were also perceived as being in continual dispute and 'obstruction' of each other.
2. The Internal Services team leader had taken out a bullying complaint against the new services section manager. The complaint had not been upheld and this had not resolved the situation.
3. Within the Internal Services team one female member had taken out a bullying grievance against her section manager, and was being urged by friends in the team to do the same in relation to a younger team member whom she claimed had continually harassed her.

The situation

The initial brief came from the commissioning divisional manager through HR. This line manager was responsible for the whole Internal Services and Customer Services division. The two teams that were the cause of his concern were Internal and Customer Services.

The two service teams were interdependent – having to pass concerns and work backwards and forwards within the group – and each had its own team manager reporting to the joint services section manager, who had been in post over a period of some six months.

Neither the service teams nor their management were functioning. Emotions were running high, and inter-team complaints, allegations and talk of grievances were rife. The commissioning manager now saw mediation as a last chance for the services section to solve its own problems before he had to intervene unilaterally to make personnel and management changes to prevent lasting business damage in what was fast becoming an irretrievable situation.

It was clear from the outset that more than one experienced facilitator would be needed and that sound consultancy judgement and skills would be required from the start in order to ensure the viability and design of the mediation. This involved exploring the initial perceptions and expectations of all the parties, including the commissioning manager. The mediation was undertaken on this occasion by the authors co-mediating together.

As we deepened our initial discussions, it was apparent not only that the teams were evidently conflicting in their everyday tasks and relationships but also that the two team leaders were in direct conflict with each other and that both had fallen out with the new services section manager. It was therefore necessary to go through a lengthy procedure with all concerned to ensure that the decision to enter mediation was agreed across the group, was voluntary and was understood.

Mediation set-up

The first thing to note about a larger inter-team mediation – as opposed to a pair or small group mediation – is that it is complex and requires a very thorough initial briefing, consultation and careful design at the point of set-up.

By the end of a week of consultation we had established willingness across the managers and their teams for giving mediation a try. This information process had included a circular e-mail to all participants answering some of their queries and outlining in more detail the nature, goals and process of the proposed inter-team mediation event.

We always make clear when introducing mediation that the participants are not signing up to a belief that the mediation *will work*, only to their wish for an *improvement in their situation* and their *willingness to give the process of mediation a try*.

With the commissioning manager we were clear that we would conduct our work in two stages for which we would need between one and four days of agreed work and the availability of those involved. The first stage would involve our assessment of the suitability of the situation for mediation and the formation of a suitable design. Depending on our findings the second stage would be the facilitation of the full inter-team mediation.

The team mediation

Individual meetings

The plan that we confirmed with HR and with all managers concerned was that we would hold individual mediation meetings with the team managers on the first day, followed by individual meetings held across the teams on the following two days. At the end of this process we would report back to the commissioning manager on the viability of running an inter-team mediation day.

As it turned out we altered our plan as a result of our initial individual meetings with the management team. Although it was clear that the team problems were real – and had indeed become entrenched – it was equally clear that the management team were in deadlock and that this in turn was complicating and reinforcing the team divide. The added complication was that members of the management team were dubious about being able to resolve their difficulties, and when we suggested that we address their conflict prior to the main mediation event, they were undecided.

By the end of our first day's work, then, we were back with the commissioning divisional manager to say that we could see no way in which an inter-team mediation could be effective without first addressing the conflicts within the management team – but that his managers were divided about this proposal.

After some discussion, which included the divisional manager, the services management team decided that they would give mediation a chance, as it was the only alternative left to them through which they could stay in control of their destinies.

The team managers' mediation day

The resulting management team mediation took a full day and, in point of fact, achieved a valuable result. The work was by no means simple but, as is often the case, the fear and projections that had built up around the personal differences and conflicted views were, in the end, far less catastrophic than anticipated. Once the more difficult perceptions were shared then a certain solidarity emerged between the two team-leaders, who now saw that both they and their teams were equally threatened. This new 'rapprochement in hardship' created the room to share common concerns as to how to reconcile their teams and to protect their vulnerable team members, who they feared could be threatened by the inter-team event.

By the end of the day a number of important things had been achieved: the management team had assumed responsibility for the future well-being of their teams and this had allowed them to resolve some of their more superficial differences and to focus away from their disagreements and to look productively at common shared performance issues.

There was also some difficult personal ground to cover in addressing the grievance brought previously by the team leader of Internal Services against the new section manager, but this was reviewed in a growing atmosphere of greater understanding and the shared threat of failure to all their interests. The new section manager also had the opportunity to clarify his position in a more personal way than previously, and to re-establish something of his authority.

The agreements reached were largely to do with arranging early communication in the future to prevent wrong assumptions, together with a resolve to keep sharing perceptions and to examine both personal and team differences and needs. Perhaps the most influential agreement of the day was that the management team would share at the inter-team mediation the fact that they had now reached a number of agreements of their own and that they would now be looking to support their teams to do the same.

Clearly this was a very powerful first gain in that it offered an example of reconciliation and agreement to their team members. During our individual meetings with the rest of the team members it was clear how important those gains would be as the common complaint was: 'how can the teams be expected to agree if the managers are in conflict?'

The full inter-team mediation day

The gains made with the management team did not, however, remove the considerable difficulties that we anticipated in running the inter-team event. The main problem – which we had to plan for in detail – concerned the historical sub-groupings, together with the very high levels of emotionality and reactivity and, in some cases, vulnerability that had built up over time.

As we started the inter-team mediation day we felt that between the mediation with the managers and the preparatory work with the team we had already covered something of a 'marathon'. However it was this very preparatory hard work that had set in motion the process of reflection and adjustment that, as it turned out, was achieved more easily than we, or the teams, might have anticipated.

The major shift in the event was accomplished in the very first part of the day when the managers in turn reported back to the group on their agreed disclosure about their own mediation and the shape of the agreements that they had reached together.

This had two effects: first, there was palpable relief in the group, and second, this move allowed the managers themselves to go into a more supportive and facilitative role with their teams and to encourage them in their endeavours to achieve their own agreements. Clearly what had impacted negatively on both teams was the lack of overall strategy and communication of the managers, who were blocked by their own personal differences. This first evidence of their new agreements – around overall strategy and planning – therefore made an immediate and significant difference to the teams and to the success of the mediation.

We did, as anticipated, have high emotions to deal with in the course of the event and we did variously use 'time outs' and allow space for the 'sub-groupings' to emerge around age and working style. These were adequately 'ventilated', acknowledged and the underlying issues gradually identified and listed.

By the end of the day, the agreement reached was actually a quite detailed and complex one. Predictably several agreements were about communications: to be respectful, avoid gossip and incorporate ways to make early statements in future of difficulties or problems within or between the teams.

There were other agreements relating to an improved system for team meetings, including a forum for sharing successes and for accentuating positives between the teams. There was even a joint 'road show' planned to communicate across the larger group the work and the services available from the service teams and to help profile the two teams to the whole group as newly combining in a more positive collaboration.

Finally, there was an interesting acknowledgment of the process of mediation in the stated agreement 'to seek out third parties *to mediate* in early stages of any future potential disagreement'.

This was perhaps an implicit vote of confidence in the lengthy but successful process that they had undertaken together over the four days of this intensive mediation initiative.

Chapter 10: The essentials

Team mediation can encompass multiple difficulties, personal sub-conflicts and grievances within a team, department or group of people. In this chapter, we have detailed two typical case studies of team mediation.

The recounting of these team mediation case studies shows how multi-faceted they can be and reflects their complexity.

A structured and safe mediation can really help a team deal with the underlying issues between its members by open discussion and skilled help from the mediators to decide on their own solutions and better ways forward.

11
Case studies of workplace mediation for boardroom conflicts

Conflict in the boardroom can have severe consequences; it not only has an almost immediate negative effect on profits or share prices but can threaten the very survival of a business. If directors who are in conflict or in power struggles with each other actually want to find a way to resolve problems, then mediation is an option they should certainly consider. A confidential means of having their discussions facilitated by someone skilled at mediation and not taking sides could be in the interests of them both, as well as of the long-term future of the company.

MEDIATION FOR A FAMILY MANUFACTURING FIRM BETWEEN DIRECTORS – FATHER AND SON

Conflicts are difficult enough in themselves, but add in the complexities and emotions of a family with its issues of interdependence, control and family dynamics, then mediators really do have to work for their money! Let us give you the following example of a mediation for a family company.

Jo Morris set up a manufacturing company in Birmingham (making tools for the car industry) over 20 years ago and built it up very successfully to an annual turnover of £5.5 million. He was now in his late 50s and was chairman of the company. His son, Terry Morris, had worked for the company since he left school, and had been managing director for three years. They also had four other directors on the board and one non-executive director.

Father and son had always experienced a difficult relationship with each other. Terry found his father overly domineering and controlling, and Jo thought his son was too disorganized, too risk taking. The situation came to a head when the profits of the company began to spiral downwards (at a time when the car industry generally went through difficult times). Terry desperately wanted to find a way of diversifying their manufacturing base into a whole new field, which meant a significant new investment in tool-making machinery. His father fundamentally disagreed with this and wanted to continue as they were.

Terry spent some time lobbying and speaking to the other directors explaining why he thought this had to happen. In a boardroom meeting a week later, however, the whole situation blew up into a huge row between father and son as their disagreement escalated in front of the whole board. Jo suddenly got angry with his son and basically said in a loud voice that he was in charge whether Terry liked it or not. Terry stormed out of the room, leaving the remaining directors at a loss in terms of what to say or do.

That something had to be done was clear. This destabilization at the top of the company was already causing confusion and delayed decision making. One of the directors, the finance director, took it upon herself to have a private word with first Jo and then Terry.

There was a lot of strong feeling on both sides, and each felt betrayed by the other. The finance director, Alison, knew about mediation and what it was – and asked both of them whether they saw this as a way out of their mutual difficulties as well as a means of helping them make some crucial decisions concerning the future of the company.

Neither was interested in the possibility of mediation initially but, after a couple of days had passed, Terry approached his father and said if they did not sort this out and go for mediation together, then he was going to hand in his resignation. To cut a long story short, they decided to give mediation a go, and contacted an independent mediation company. The mediation was arranged for the following week and took two days of solid discussion before they came anywhere near finding a solution that they could both agree to.

The discussions were long and difficult but, in brief, Jo agreed in the end to invest in the new tool machinery and to test this as a way forward. Terry in return agreed to structured financial accounting and regular accounting feedback. There were other important agreements made, but these were the main ones – the ones that, in fact, got them 'unstuck' and avoided what would have been an inevitable and severe financial loss for their family company.

MEDIATION FOR AN INTERNATIONAL COMPANY BETWEEN THE CHAIRMAN AND THE MANAGING DIRECTOR

Here is an example of a major conflict between a long-standing chairman of an international company and a new managing director.

This particular international company manufactured metal components for a wide range of industries and had a number of production plants worldwide, with a total turnover of around £250 million. For some years, as the company continued to grow, the chairman had the dual role of chairman of the board and managing director (not an ideal situation – to have both roles) until one day he decided to invite one of the more successful of the regional managers to move to the UK and become managing director of the whole company.

While both were very able and competent men, their relationship was strained from the start. Their personalities and their communication styles were very different. The chairman was public-school educated and, while very dedicated to the business, was also quite rigid and inflexible and liked to do things in a particular way. The managing director was a self-made man brought up in the United States, very active, highly successful and very direct and outspoken. Conflict soon emerged between them when it became apparent that the chairman continued to have contact with regional plant managers and to be directly involved in future projects and decisions in expanding the manufacturing facilities worldwide (in other words, he was continuing to involve himself in decisions that were now the remit of the MD).

Their conflict was felt in the boardroom meetings right from the beginning, not so much by their losing their temper or anything so overt but rather because the tension between them was palpable, as well as the way they had differences of opinion. It became visible to everyone that their relationship was in difficulties. As some months went by, it became clear that what was happening between them was having a very detrimental and damaging effect on the business, and in particular on the senior level of management: some of the directors began to take sides, making alliances with one or the other, causing disharmony and confusion throughout the whole company.

In this case, it was their legal advisor who introduced them to the possibility of a confidential mediation, and they found a suitably experienced and qualified workplace mediation consultant. The mediation did in fact take place over a whole day but it did not end in the usual way.

While they had some very useful and frank discussions during the mediation meeting, the end result of the mediation was that the chairman, after much deliberation and thought, took an important decision; he decided to hand in his resignation and take a well-earned retirement. What made a significant difference (as opposed to sudden departures due to irreconcilable differences between directors or senior management) was that they were able to use the facilitated mediation to carefully plan the details of this departure of the chairman in a way that was in the best interests not only of the chairman but of the company, its employees and its shareholders. They did this amicably and with mutual respect.

Chapter 11: The essentials

Boardroom conflict and personal power struggles can threaten the whole survival of a company. This chapter gives a case study of a conflict between father and son in a family-owned company, and a conflict between a chairman and managing director in a large international company.

If a director wants to find a workable solution and is willing to talk to the other person – facilitated by a skilled mediator – then a confidential mediation can be very appropriate and ways forward can be ironed out to the advantage of those involved as well as for the organization and shareholders.

PART III

The philosophy and processes of mediation:

in support of conflict managers and organizational development

In Part III we shall first look to deepen our terms of reference on the nature and workings of interpersonal conflict and then to offer managers formats for responding to conflict and for quickly resolving everyday conflicts using the Brief Mediation™ model.

We shall conclude by exploring the possibility of responding to the 21st-century identity crisis of business and organizations by generating empowered and consensus-based working cultures based upon the philosophy, processes and tools 'beyond mediation'.

12

Why do conflicts arise?

Some universal, individual and interpersonal models

In this chapter we shall be looking in more depth at the physiology, psychology and interpersonal dynamics that underlie or accompany interpersonal conflict. The purpose of this exploration is to help understand something of the universality of conflict, the role of individual 'maps' of perception, the effects of change and stress in business life and the variety of manifestation and tactics that conflict can assume. Our exploration of these models is intended to help the mediator and the first-line conflict manager to better understand the dynamics of those in conflict and to avoid being drawn into negative attitudes or destructive behaviours.

STRESS, THREAT AND CONFLICT: 'HARDWIRED FOR A FIGHT ...'

We shall begin our exploration by looking at models from neurology and physiology that contribute to our understanding of both the universality and the emergence of conflict. We shall do this with special reference to the conditions of continuous change that exacerbate our stress within the contemporary climate of business change. There is currently much attention being paid to workplace stress, but its fundamental relationship to conflict is not often understood.

In examining the physiological models of stress and conflict we shall draw upon the significant work of Hans Selye MD, the originator of modern stress theory whose research and book *The Stress of Life* have played a significant role in understanding the mind–body links in modern psychosomatic medicine.

The mechanics of stress are 'hardwired' and universal. When any source of threat is presented to the organism, the brain stem initiates a succession of hormonal releases that mobilize the whole body into what is referred to as the *alarm response*, which in turn instigates the full antagonistic *fight–flight* process that lies at the heart of the *stress response* (Figure 12.1). There is also the commonly seen *freeze* response, where the victim stands still, does nothing and 'shuts down' until the threat is over. In essence, this hardwired process ensures that the organism is poised and energized to do one of two things: to resist or to flee. This mobilization is neither voluntary nor rational – it is dictated at a basic physiological level by the imperative of the survival of the organism.

Hans Selye, writing in *The Stress of Life*, sees this process as both a behavioural and a biological one: 'There are two principle ways of defending yourself against aggression: to advance and to attack the foe or to retreat

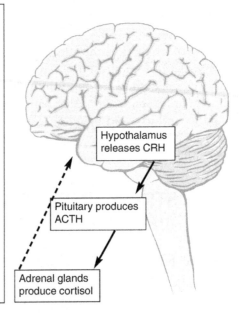

This diagram shows the steps involved in what Selye describes as the brain's 'antagonistic' defence against threat or aggression, composed of a dual arousal and calming mechanism.

The arousal originates in the hypothalamus where the CRH (corticotrophin-releasing hormone) is released to the pituitary gland, which in turn produces ACTH (adrenocorticotropic hormone).

The end point of this sequence is the stimulation of the adrenal glands by the ACTH to manufacture and release cortisol, which is released throughout the body – including to the hypothalamus where it balances and counters the stress-producing release.

'This ingenious negative-feedback effect of Cortisol is what prevents the stress response from spiralling out of control' (Sternberg, 2000: 58).

Hypothalamus releases CRH

Pituitary produces ACTH

Adrenal glands produce cortisol

Figure 12.1 The brain's stress-response mechanism
Source: Sternberg, 2000

and run out of his reach. Both these techniques are also used by the defensive forces of our tissues against foes inside the body' (Selye, 1956: 89).

The universal stress response is one that we share with all the animal kingdom and there is clearly great survival value in this automatic reaction. The additional complexity of human conflict, however, arises when the higher brain interprets the sensory signals that it receives not just as threats to our physical safety but also as psychological threats affecting our needs, values or our identity. The _key variable_ in human conflict then – and the accompanying emotions of fear that surround it – is to be found in _perception_.

Whereas most of us will face significantly fewer physical threats in the course of our lives than did our original ancestors, our physiological and psychological systems are likely to be equally stressed on a daily basis by the simple _psychological perception of threat_.

> Our perception of stress, and therefore our response to it, is an ever-changing thing... It depends on previous experience and knowledge, as well as on the actual event that has occurred. And it depends on memory too. A memory is not a threat – it cannot kill or harm, and yet a memory of a stressful event can turn on the stress response almost as much as the original event itself.
>
> (Sternberg, 2000: 121).

Understanding this basic physio/psychological phenomenon is important to understanding the dynamics of conflict and offers managers valuable information in the context both of change management and of the best approach to breakdowns in working relationships.

STRESS AND CONFLICT IN THE CONTEMPORARY BUSINESS ENVIRONMENT OF CHANGE

A further dimension to workplace conflict can be found in the link between cumulative change and the phenomenon of personal and group stress that has become so endemic in contemporary individual, family and working life.

According to Hans Selye, whether or not our stress levels become destructive or remain manageable is dependent on two factors: the degree of cumulative change that we experience and the degree to which we are in control of our mind, feelings, resources, skills and outcomes. To be overwhelmed with the stimulation and demands of change and to lack the control and the internal or external resources to cope is to court danger and to push the natural GAS – the general adaptation syndrome identified by Selye in his research – into its destructive phase of 'exhaustion'.

This physiological model of stress holds true also for modern organizations that have constantly to adapt to the multiple pressures of the markets, competition, new technology and the demands of quality, costs, speed, flexibility and service standards. In Figure 12.2 we have included a diagnostic model that is particularly relevant to first-line conflict managers and to mediators in assessing the links between ongoing *change, stress* and individual or group *control*. The model also indicates what kinds of conflicts result when people are insufficiently regarded or resourced to be able to accommodate the demands of changes that they perceive to threaten their interests or their well-being.

The two axes of this model derive from Selye's insights and indicate: the *level and rate of change* and the *level of internal and external control* experienced by those involved in situations of change. Together, these dictate the levels of stress experienced. The four resulting quadrants of the model also contain an indication as to how *conflict* may come to be manifest in relation to both these sets of criteria and the progressive progress of individual or group stress.

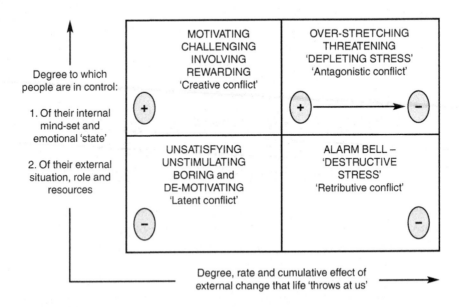

Figure 12.2 Diagnostic stress, change and conflict management reference model

© MCRG 2007

In conclusion, then, we can say that we now inhabit a working environ-ment that is, by the nature of its inherent climate of multiple pressure and change, increasingly stressful and potentially not simply a danger to health and well-being but a major contributory factor in the escalation of individual and group conflict.

INDIVIDUAL PERCEPTION, LIFE-STANCES AND CONFLICT

We move next from the universals underlying personal conflict to the psychological triggers of individual and interpersonal conflict. What we are asking here is:

> What is it that dictates whether an individual's adaptive reactions to change and to the 'stress of life' remain balanced and positive, or whether stress results in overload, in decreased performance and in the psychological conditions for conflict and the breakdown of relationships in the workplace?

We shall examine two psychological perspectives: namely, our individual 'mental maps' and our attitudes to ourselves and others manifested in our individual life-stances.

Our personal 'mental maps'

We all have a natural need to manage life experience by 'making sense' of the people and events that we encounter, rather than just reacting and adapting to events and to people's behaviour.

This means that everything that happens to us is related in our brain to our previous experience up to that point and is interpreted, judged and acted upon on the basis of this history. We build up a body of experience and the mental process of generalization enables us to generate beliefs and values based on our unique history. Over time our personal mental filters result in a sequence of beliefs, of reinforcing emotional states and consequently of repeated behaviours that come to form the basis of our particular 'map of reality'. This map guides our approach to life and makes predictable our typical everyday reactions and behaviours.

Clearly the mental 'maps' of different people may be incompatible. Everybody's experiential 'map of the world' and consequential beliefs are subjective and proceed from unique experiences. Hence each individual tends to think that his or her map is the unique and definitive one, and that events and people are acceptable only if they 'figure within' or are compatible with the individual's map of reality. This understanding plays a vital part in managing interpersonal conflict.

What is the value then to the mediator or conflict manager of investigating and helping those in conflict to share their perceptual maps? We have already touched upon the answer to this: essentially conflict proceeds from *the perception of threat* to one's survival, beliefs or interests. To encourage expression and understanding of the 'maps' of those in conflict helps restore the power and the leverage to listen rather than to blame and to begin to understand each other's needs and the personal threats underlying their conflict.

Our behavioural stances and 'life-positions'

So far we have focused upon the universal conflict triggers of stress and the perceptual filter of the individual's map. A model that offers additional value in describing and resolving interpersonal conflict is the 'four life positions' concept expanded by Thomas Harris (1967) in his popular work entitled *I'm OK – You're OK*.

In essence, the life-positions model starts from the premise that people are conditioned by their earliest transactions and parental 'life-scripts' to adopt one of four life-positions and that the underlying dynamics of these positions can be 'shorthanded' as a blend of the three behavioural modes of 'Parent', 'Adult' and 'Child' (the PAC from Transactional Analysis or TA originated by Eric Berne).

Harris describes four possible life-positions that people can adopt in relation to themselves and others and that have a direct bearing on the individual and interactive origins of conflict. These are summarized in the box below.

Harris's life-positions

'I'm OK – you're OK'
- I am a valuable human being, I deserve due respect and consideration and so do you.
- I will therefore be motivated to get along with you, and to go for 'what is right and fair' for us both.

'I'm OK – you're not OK'
- There is something wrong with you, and I do not need to treat you with respect or consideration.

■ I will be motivated to prove that you are to blame, to create complaints and ultimately to dismiss you.

'I'm not OK – you're OK'

■ There is something wrong with me; I do not deserve to be treated with respect and consideration.
■ I will be motivated to get away from you; I will accept unachievable targets, take time off, drink too much, resign and – in the extreme – move towards self-harm or illness.

'I'm not OK – you're not OK'

■ The position of futility: there is no way out.
■ In the extreme – 'everyone is wrong and everyone is damned'.

The life-positions tend to be associated with characteristic behaviours and attitudes. Each behavioural style has strengths and weaknesses. Where conflict is occurring the negative aspects of each style are evident and the focus here is on the negative aspects.

Parent

There are two expressions of the 'Parent' described in the TA model: the 'Nurturing Parent' and the 'Critical or Controlling Parent'. Parent behaviours are characterized by strong one-way value judgements.

The positive use of the Critical Parent response is when the other genuinely needs information, guidelines or boundaries – as with a real child or someone in a learning situation. The intent is to enhance the other's skill and independence.

The negative Critical Parent behaviours come from values, judgements or behaviours in line with the life-position: 'I'm OK, you're not OK'. The person operating from this position will look to dictate outcomes and to proscribe actions on the basis of a position of _self-assumed_ 'rightness' and prerogative. The intent, whether conscious or unconscious, is to limit or even undermine the other's competence and autonomy.

Nurturing Parent behaviour, looking after another, is usually more comfortable to live with. The negative aspect involves overprotecting, or sorting out other people's problems for them, even if they resent it or would be better off being given the opportunity to learn. This also involves the 'I'm OK you're not OK' position, but this time in the form 'you would be lost without me'.

In terms of interactive outcomes, both Parent behaviours will tend to promote win–lose outcomes where the dominant party gains at the expense of the other. Although the controlling or critical parent demon-strates visibly negative behaviours both of these 'parental' modes in fact can imply win–lose outcomes because of behaviours that 'control' and hence disempower the other.

Child

'Free Child' behaviours are identified as 'paralleling the behaviour of a child who is not adapting to the demands and constraints of an adult'. The positive aspects are curiosity, excitement, spontaneity and playfulness. The negative ones are selfishness and recklessness. The positive Free Child behaviours are often perceived as 'inferior' to the logical and pragmatic dictates of contemporary working life and society. However in recent years there has been a re-evaluation of spontaneous, intuitive processes and of EQ or 'emotional quotient'. This revaluation includes access to what it often termed our 'inner child', and 'freeing the inner child' is seen as regaining personal spontaneity, creativity and the fun of life.

'Adapted Child' behaviours are very common. We have all been trained to be polite, to say please and thank-you, to queue, to share and so forth; our parents went to a lot of effort to train us so that those responses became routine. The negative aspects of Adapted Child behaviour are either an excessive compliance to the demands of others, or automatic resistance to the demands of others. It is also worth noting that the Child always perceives 'the big people' – their 'superiors' – as making unrea-sonable 'demands' on them or 'telling them what to do'.

Over-compliant Child behaviour usually reflects the life-position 'I'm not OK, you're OK' – so I must do everything to keep your approval, whatever the cost. Where the pressures or requests are resented and responded to in a passive-aggressive way, the stance can be 'I'm OK, you're not OK' for making all those unreasonable demands on me.

These 'deferential' or 'rebellious' positions have their origins in the way the person handled 'dependency' in childhood. People replay the early childhood style of relationships rather than responding in a constructive adaptive way to the present situation.

Adult

'Adult' describes values, judgements or behaviours that are a response to present-time realities, that operate with objective, factually-based judge-ments and equate with the life-position: 'I'm OK – you're OK'.

The Adult stance then is 'higher-brain' managed and is primarily concerned with facts, choices, possibilities and outcomes. Importantly – in terms of interpersonal relations – the Adult operates with an equal awareness of 'the other' – treated not as an object but as a real, potentially positive and therefore welcome part of all shared outcomes.

It is through utilizing Adult perspectives and behaviours that the win–win outcomes inherent in the shared experience of 'OK-ness' are achieved.

Clearly conflict and aggression can originate and be fed by the behaviours and resulting win–lose life-positions of the parties involved. This is true where either the Critical Parent or the Adapted Child behaviour is involved.

TA also offers another useful description of the dynamic of conflict by asserting that where transactions between these ego states are 'complementary' then a mutually acceptable conclusion will be achieved. In contrast, where transactions are 'crossed' then either one of the parties involved has to 'lose' by adapting their behaviours to the other or the result will be a direct conflict.

Clearly there is much mileage in both the dynamic understandings and the descriptive language of TA and we shall build upon this first description by extending our focus in the following sections to consider 'conflict style' and 'conflict tactics'.

PERSONAL RESPONSES TO CONFLICT: PASSIVE/AGGRESSIVE/ASSERTIVE

A useful progression in our understanding of conflict at this point may be had from considering the description in contemporary Assertion Theory of the various personality types and stances involved in aggression and conflict.

Assertion trainers tend to categorize people's responses to fulfilling their needs in relation to others by describing four personality types. These will be outlined below with parallel references to previous models.

The aggressive personality or stance

This is based on the demand that others conform to the aggressor's wishes and needs and relinquish their map and needs in the situation. The intention of aggressive persons is to secure their own needs by control over the other and thus to get their way. They utilize behaviours that are angry, pushy, bullying, intimidating and that involve self-aggrandizement – essentially achieved at the expense of those around them. In TA terms these are highly negative Critical Parent behaviours in line with the fight strategy that demonstrate an 'I'm OK – you're not OK' life-position and seek to achieve win–lose outcomes.

The passive personality or stance

This demonstrates, by contrast, attitudes of fearfulness and timidity (the flight stance in the face of aggression or conflict) and will tend to seek 'peace at any price' and choose strategies of self-negation, self-sacrifice and submission. The passive utilizes behaviours of compliance, conformity and over-pleasing to achieve safety and protect his or her position, and is happy to accept a 'lose–win' in order to preserve the peace or to win protection or favour.

Passives may also use withdrawal, avoidance, non-communication, repression and depression, and may even fall into (adopt) psychosomatic illnesses as an alternative to facing conflict. In TA terms the behaviours are Adapted Child and the lose–win outcome that is experienced fulfils the accompanying belief that 'I'm not OK – you're OK'.

The passive-aggressive personality or stance

Here the passive person makes a bid for his or her own form of control without confrontation by employing passive-aggressive strategies and the behaviours of manipulation, charm or victimhood.

In this stance, although the behaviours appear and are ostensibly compliant, the sub-text and the longer-term gambit are to oblige the opposition to comply with the passive-aggressive's own needs and agendas either by blackmail or through guilt. Passive-aggressives get their way by the kind of indirect sabotage or non-cooperation that is very hard to put your finger on or to prove.

The assertive personality or stance

The assertive personality, by contrast, is characterized by present-time rationality and a considered concern for people that involves the understanding and recognition of the needs of both the self and others.

The behaviours associated with the assertive stance then are interpersonal negotiation of needs, issues and boundaries. The style of assertive communication demonstrates a reasoned, respectful willingness to interact when in conflict with the aim of achieving solutions offering mutual benefit and shared gain.

Over time, assertive relationships result in attitudes and practices of cooperation, fairness and consensus decision making that are the special mark of
assertive relationships, families or working environments. The assertive
person is thus able to say and mean: 'I want what is fair for both of us.'

In TA terms, this assertive personality corresponds to Adult behaviour
and seeks outcomes based upon a script of 'I'm OK – you're OK' as the
basis for win–win outcomes and conflict resolution.

Table 12.1 brings together for reference the descriptions of both TA and
Assertion Theory set against their anticipated win–lose outcomes.

INTERPERSONAL CONFLICT STYLES AND TACTICS: A SUMMARY

Within the development of human relations psychology, much attention
has also been devoted from the 1960s onwards to 'styles of conflict' and to
instruments of measurement designed to profile interactive conflict.

Table 12.1 Correlation of personality descriptions from contemporary
Assertion Theory and TA, showing win–lose outcomes

Assertion and TA personality descriptions	Strategy and values	Typical behaviours	Associated emotions	Win–lose outcome
'Aggressive' stance 'Critical Parent'	Dominance Control Competition Force	Controlling Tense/driven Dictating	Fight Frustration Anger	Seeks an outright **win–lose** to impose their agenda
'Passive' stance 'Adapted Negative Child'	Peace Understanding Acceptance Non-engagement	Placatory Deferential Avoiding	Fear Denial Self-depreciation	Expects or will tolerate **lose–win** to obtain acceptance
'Passive-aggressive' stance 'Rebellious Adapted Child'	Hidden control Duplicity Factions Sabotage	Scheming Manipulation and indirect undermining	Resentment Repression Revenge	Will accept **lose–win** as a step to a revenge win–lose
'Assertive' stance 'Adult'	Respect Openness Dialogue Problem-solving	Disclosure Enquiry Validation Negotiation	Centredness Empathy Positive regard	Seeks a **win–win** for mutual gain and long-term relationship gains

Blake and Mouton (1964) originated the idea of conflict styles, and Ruble and Thomas (1976) delineated five conflict styles that are differentiated by their somewhat different definition of 'assertiveness' (by which is understood behaviours directed to satisfying one's own concerns) and 'cooperativeness' (by which is understood behaviours directed to satisfying the other's concerns).

We have restricted ourselves at this point to a comparative table with which to close this section. Table 12.2 describes some of the tactics and strategies of conflict and may be of value for both the mediator and the manager or HR consultant as a summary of some of the common behavioural tactics manifested in conflict situations. These are again grouped with reference to our ongoing descriptions from Assertion Theory, OK life positions and TA.

Table 12.2 Conflict tactics set against Assertion Theory and TA descriptions

Style	Tactic	Pitch	Goal
'Aggressive' stance 'Critical Parent'	Adopt a fixed position	'We don't move on this.'	Enforced compliance
	Issues threats	'If demands are not met, then…'	Dominance
	Irrevocable action	'Call your bluff.'	Capitulation
	Ridicule, jokes, insults	'How stupid is that?'	Belittle or discredit the opposition
	Violence, damage	'An offer you can't refuse.'	Fear
	Multiple warheads – attack on all fronts	'You won't know what's hit you.'	Confusion and overload
	Pull rank	'What I say goes.'	Overrule
	Blind with science	'Can't be done.'	Dominate by expertise
	Tit for tat	'Take that!'	Muscle flexing
	The pre-emptive strike	'I'm that dangerous!'	Awe, fear
	Invoke (favourable) higher ruling	'They must decide.'	Power lobby
'Passive' stance 'Adapted Negative Child'	Change the subject	'Let's move on.'	Avoidance
	Avoid, withdraw	'Can we return to this another time?'	Delay
	Placatory gifts	'Be nice to me.'	Subordination
	Belly up	'Do what you want.'	Pity or support

Style	Tactic →	Pitch →	Goal
'Passive-aggressive' stance 'Rebellious Adapted Child'	Guilt trip	'If you valued me...'	Compliance through guilt
	Self-hurt	'Now look what you've done.'	Revenge
	Malignment	'Who is the real villain here?'	Power reversal
	Blackmail	'You wouldn't want this to come out.'	Power reversal
	Muddy the waters	'The issue is not simple.'	Confuse, diffuse the force
	Invoke history and favours	'You can't do this to me.'	Manipulation
	Set the dogs on them enlist enemies	'I can't control them.'	Indirect aggression
	Spin – change the ground and focus	'There really is no problem.'	'Sleight of tongue' power
	Vilification, slander	'What kind of person would...?'	Destroying the others' moral ground
	Shape changer	'Now you see me now you don't.'	Confusion of the rules, terms, operating style
	Lackey	'I really admire....'	Alliance by servility, flattery
'Assertive' stance ' 'Adult'	Breakthrough	'What if we were to...?'	Creative solution
	Seek the high ground	'What really matters here?'	Normative solutions
	Uncover the shared ground	'What is it that we both want here?'	Cooperative solutions
	Quid pro quo	'If we were to give on this....'	Trade-offs
	Rational analysis	'Let's establish the issues.'	Problem definition
	Negative enquiry	'How is it that this damages you?'	Empathic understanding
	Consider options	'What are the possibilities here?'	Creative problem solving
	Meta-analysis	'Can we look at how we are addressing this?'	Increasing awareness and quality of process
	The big picture	'How is this problem affecting others?'	Expanding or reframing the conflict
	Good people	'What is the right thing here?'	Moral reframing
	Positive intention	'What is our real aim?'	Reframing goals as shared ground
	Go for the win–win	'So what would be good for us both?'	Positive and lasting solutions
	Third party	'Who can we trust to facilitate our outcome?'	Mediated or facilitated outcomes

AVOIDING NEGATIVITY FOR MEDIATORS AND CONFLICT MANAGERS

We shall conclude our exploration of the deeper dimensions of conflict by summarizing the position that all mediators and conflict managers need to adopt in order to remain free from the negative psychology and dynamics of conflict.

The mediation process clearly cuts across the whole dynamic of the negative position of 'I'm OK – you're not OK' both in its processes and in the attitude and skills of the mediator. By adopting Adult perspective and behaviours, the mediator refuses to enter into any of the negative judgemental, passive or punishing behaviours of the disputants and maintains a position of impartiality and fairness throughout the whole mediation process.

Neither the mediator nor the manager can work from within the dynamics of those in conflict and must step outside this frame to draw the participants onto the positive and productive ground of facts, objectivity, listening and sharing – as a gateway to new and productive alternatives to their fixed negative positions.

The essential difference that keeps the mediator and manager outside the conflict loop is the fundamental position of 'OK-ness' that they look to maintain within themselves and that they demonstrate towards others in both their attitude and skills. Sound mediation and effective conflict resolution are both based upon seeing and treating all the parties involved as being 'OK'.

By retaining his or her own 'OK-ness' the mediator or manager is empowered to maintain a positive and impartial attitude and to genuinely help those involved to make the transition from negative feelings, judgements, blame or excuses into the direction of facts, issues, needs and solutions.

The mediator is obviously supported in this task by the logic and process of the six-step model of mediation. The mediation process clearly progresses from the acknowledgment of each person's story, position and concerns to the wholly Adult ground of the identification of common issues and the generation of creative solutions that offer real gain to all parties.

For the conflict manager there are also supports and formats that can offer similar structure and guidance, and we shall examine some of these communication techniques and skills in the next chapter.

Chapter 12: The essentials

Human beings are 'hardwired' for instinctual flight or fight when threatened by conflict. It is our perception of a situation that determines whether this natural and primitive reaction results in negative or positive effects.

The human being can only absorb so much stress, especially when it is continuous or out of our control. Given the present pace of life, most of us inhabit a working environment that is inherently stressful and potentially harmful to our health and well-being. The effects of poor organizational change can surface as 'shortened fuses' and be manifest in increased interpersonal and group conflicts.

Our mental filters create our own maps of reality, which we experience as real and as the only way to see things.

The behavioural descriptions of Parent, Child and Adult from TA, and their associated 'life-positions' in the Thomas Harris model, can also explain why so much of our communication with each other can end up in misunderstandings and 'crossed wires' or in outcomes that fall short of win–win.

The task of both the mediator and the conflict manager is to retain their own 'OK-ness' and from this positive position to help others to achieve the transition to the Adult ground of facts, issues and needs that can lead to a fuller understanding and can pave the way to new alternatives and agreements.

13

Why and how should managers respond to conflict?

Successful conflict management in the workplace depends initially on the attitude, understanding and skills of first-line managers and their willingness to respond to conflict. This is clearly not an easy task; as we have seen the pace of modern business and organizational change, market and customer demands and the growing complexity of work roles and tasks mean that managers have to keep many balls in the air and need to be equipped with a large range of process and people skills.

Traditionally managers have been trained and equipped primarily to deliver results around systems of 'performance management', and hence many managers feel some trepidation when they encounter employees with issues such as personal distress, mental health concerns, work-related stress and, of course, in the demanding area of *conflict prevention and conflict de-escalation*. The demands of our compensation culture add even more pressure on an already overworked or overstretched management.

In this chapter we shall both examine the reasons for managers to address workplace conflict and offer five effective formats that may prove useful for them in the task of conflict resolution and prevention.

'CONFLICT COSTS': MANAGING CONFLICT EFFECTIVELY SAVES MONEY

First, why should managers be especially interested in the prevention, management and resolution of conflict? The answer is basically that 'conflict costs' – and its costs are not only significant but appear presently to be growing year on year. Conflict is one of industry's most hidden costs, and yet is the least costly to remedy.

We have already touched upon the constituent elements of the 'cost of conflict' in Chapter 1, and noted that in the UK the government has repeatedly urged employers to resolve workplace conflict 'early and informally' in line with some of the best current practice cited from the United States, Australia and New Zealand.

The hidden price of workplace conflict for managers is the amount of management time (including that of senior managers and directors who may be called in) that can be tied up with complex 'people' complaints – valuable time and energy that would be better spent on work tasks or in creating improved quality or productivity. It has been estimated that more than 20 per cent of managers' time can be taken up with handling conflicts or differences of one kind or another and, for some industrial sectors, this may be an underestimate.

In our experience, managers with the will, awareness and skills to defuse a difficult situation – before it escalates into a complaint – could deal with a large percentage of the workplace conflicts that are either eventually referred to professional mediators or that actually end up at formal investigations or before employment tribunals.

So the first and simplest rationale for the manager to take conflict resolution seriously is that conflict costs – and that, by early and skilled intervention, managers can save significant costs and resources. This saving should be measured not only in financial terms but also in preserving individual and team morale, well-being and work satisfaction.

ANGER AND HOW TO HANDLE IT

Anger is undoubtedly one of the most disturbing of emotions to deal with, especially when it is directed at you personally. Angry or aggressive reactions in the workplace can come from any direction – from work colleagues, managers, clients, customers, suppliers or staff in different departments.

Unlike tears or grief, for which you can pass the tissues, or a sudden discharge of laughter, which is excellent at releasing tension, anger can be volatile, threatening and intimidating. It is loaded with untold tension and the impulse to attack or judge another.

If you are at the receiving end of an aggressive outburst, it can be quite shocking and unnerving, and in these changing and stressful times it is most likely that you will have to deal with this sooner or later, if not every day. The question is: how do you deal with it and still maintain your professionalism as a manager?

When faced with anger in your private life, you may choose to react angrily yourself and just say what you want to say, but in the workplace you cannot do this. You need to find a way of responding to someone's anger that results in your remaining professional and respectful and, at the same time, enables you to defuse the strong feelings and manage the dialogue so that the interaction remains as constructive as possible.

Very few people are skilled at handling anger. Most managers handle it well enough but some deal with it poorly or bluff their way through and hope for the best, learning by trial and error. Faced with anger, people tend to:

- get angry themselves and retaliate;
- go on the defensive and come up with excuses as to why they did what they did;
- go off on totally unrelated, tangential stories about something or other;
- blame someone else;
- say nothing, look blank and hope it all goes away.

Whatever the response, all of the above will most likely make the other person even more angry or frustrated, thus escalating the bad feeling and provoking even higher levels of irritation and verbal aggression.

Most people get angry because they are *upset about something*. This is a very simple way to put it but, in many ways, it is that simple. People get angry, and raise their voices, and pump up their bodies in order to 'show you' and demonstrate to you that they are upset by something. They raise their voices and shout and use strong language in order to bring attention to their upset or their plight. They want you to *know* how upset they are.

Basically, they want to be heard and they want some recognition of their upset. If they feel you are not listening to them or not understanding them, then they will 'up' their reaction and raise their voice even more so that you do hear them. Or even worse, if they feel you do not understand them or you are not 'getting' how upset they are, then they will automatically increase their anger and proceed to threats or even the use of physical violence.

Skills to defuse anger or aggression

▌ ***Don't take it personally*** or overreact or get aggressive yourself. Keep calm and remain respectful. Take a deep breath.

▌ ***Listen to what is being said.***
Don't interrupt or contradict them or deny their experience.
Don't be tempted to explain to them the error of their ways.

▌ ***Acknowledge what they are saying to you*** – by saying back to them the main elements of what they have said, before you say anything else:
'If I understand you correctly, you feel/think...'
or *'You are upset by...'*

▌ ***Acknowledge or validate how they are feeling*** – including the strength of their feeling, if appropriate:
'If that's what you think is happening, I can understand why you are so angry.'
'As you are so upset by this, I want to take this very seriously and do what I can to help resolve it.'

▌ ***Use a 'Break State'*** – if someone is extremely angry it may help to interrupt the escalation of the anger by changing some element in the situation. You may for example offer to sit down with the offended person or perhaps change location and go to a more private place such as your office.

▌ ***Invite discharge of feeling*** – if it feels right, give them some time to express or discharge their feelings, though not so much that they spiral deeper into their anger or distress. You could phrase it as:
'Is there anything more that you wish to say /to add?'

▌ ***Judge your moment to 'lead'*** – if they begin to repeat themselves or there is a danger of the anger increasing rather than decreasing, then assertively and calmly intervene, acknowledge what they have been saying and lead them towards finding solutions.

▌ ***Respond to the main issue/s involved.***
Agree with what you agree with.
And gently and respectfully disagree with what you disagree with.

▌ ***Don't deny what they are saying to you*** or go on the defensive.
Don't get sidetracked by more irrelevant or tangential arguments.

▌ ***Offer an apology*** – if appropriate – or suggest a solution or ask them what they think would provide a solution.

▌ ***Say what you are willing to do*** – and be specific about this.

- **Talk calmly and assertively**, repeat what you wish to say if necessary, as people experiencing strong emotions will find it hard to hear what you are saying (the 'broken record method' but only once or twice).

- **If emotions are too strong**, you may have to give people time to calm down and arrange to talk about it at another time.

- **Don't be tempted to be punitive or judgemental** around their expression of anger. If you can, accept it with compassion and give them the opportunity to calm down and re-phrase what the issues are for them.

- **As a last resort, contain and curtail** – only if the anger is way out of order or causing harm will you need to contain or curtail it in whatever way possible. Never put yourself or others in danger. Call for assistance or security.

Remember you cannot always rationalize with an irrational anger. Remain professional; do not rise to the bait or get angry yourself, but say skilfully, clearly and professionally what you need to say. Manage the dialogue so that you reassure and calm the person and redirect and lead him or her to a calmer, more constructive place.

Fortunately, most aggression in work settings takes the form of verbal or indirect passive-aggressive behaviour. Physical violence happens, of course, and the figures show that such incidents are increasing, but thankfully it is rare for workplace disagreements to turn into actual physical aggression. Most people, when questioned about this, say that they more commonly experience verbal aggression or verbal abuse in their workplace, so this is what we are concentrating on in this skills section.

Anger is an *emotion*, one of a range of human emotions. It is OK to be angry (as long as it does not end in harm to anyone else); it is not the end of the world. In fact, it is a fairly frequent and normal human response. The first thing someone wants you to do when they are displaying their anger towards you is to listen and to understand.

They want you to *understand what has upset them*, so much so that they feel they need to 'shout', raise their voices and exaggerate the strength of their case in order to get their message across. Unfortunately, most people do the opposite, when faced with anger. They try and stop the communication, they block it and instantly go into self-defence, which often means talking over the person or raising their voices themselves, which, of course, only serves to escalate the aggression.

Clearly there are no set rules on how best to handle anger, but the suggestions given on pp 157–58 may certainly help defuse a difficult situation quickly and respectfully.

MANAGING YOUR MIND-TALK

While we are considering self-possession in the face of anger and aggression we will close with the deepest potential source of a loss of equilibrium: namely, the way that conflict is created and made worse by what your mind tells you about it.

Whether you are aware of it or not, your mind is talking at you, telling you something, all your waking hours. This is what we term 'mind-talk' and others refer to as the 'inner dialogue' that goes on continuously in your mind. Sometimes we are aware of this mind-talk going on in our heads and at other times we have no idea at all that it is there. Whether we are conscious of these words in our head or not, all the time they are affecting how we think, how we feel and what opinions or judgements we form about ourselves and about others. The 'rub' of how powerful mind-talk can be is that we so easily come to think of it as the 'truth'.

Understanding how mind-talk operates will help you as a manager and will help you understand and manage your staff. Mind-talk takes you away from the actual reality.

> Habitual thought patterns are very powerful, instantaneous and spring into our mind with blinding speed. Something happens, at work for instance, and within seconds our mind tells us what it 'means' or what 'they' are up to… We grow up with constant reinforcement of this way of thinking, of believing what our mind tells us… and we don't even know its happening.
>
> (Whitten and Brown, 1981)

Even more importantly, what your mind is telling you can affect your feelings within an instant. There is a *direct link* between your mind-talk and your emotions. One minute you may be feeling fine, and then, within seconds after a particular thought comes into your head, you feel tense or unhappy or angry.

Where mind-talk remains unchallenged and unresolved the internal words used may become more generalized, extreme and fixed. Words you might use include:

- **Always** – 'They *always* do this.'
- **Never** – 'They *never* do what I ask them to do.'
- **Should** – 'They *should* get rid of that person.'
- **Must** – 'They *must* be blind or stupid to have organized it this way.'
- **All** – 'They *all* gossip about me.'

The kind of things your mind might tell you

▪ **About Yourself:**
'I am not good enough.'
'I will never be able to do this.'

▪ **About Others:**
'They are out to hurt me or make me look bad.'
'They do not respect me.'
'They are trying to get rid of me.'
'They are being completely unfair.'

▪ **About the Situation:**
'It's useless... Nothing I do makes any difference... It's hopeless.'
'Its unfair.'
'I can't work here/with them any longer.'
'I will get my own back.'

Strategies to manage your 'mind-talk'

The key to being in control of your mind-talk rather than it being in control of you is firstly:

BE AWARE of the fact it is happening.

NOTICE what your mind is actually saying to you.
Because if you do not notice what is going on in your mind, then it will have affected you and how you feel before you know it. Negative thoughts evoke negative feelings. If you do not notice it is happening, you will have no chance to change it.

And, secondly, the other major key to controlling your mind-talk is to ask yourself:

IS IT TRUE?
Very simply, ask yourself, is what my mind telling me true or not? Your mind-talk will either *be true, not true* or *you don't know*. The mind, of course, will instantly justify itself and say, 'Of course it is true', so you will need to be a little more persistent, a little more honest with yourself when you challenge what your mind is saying to you.

REFRAMING INFLAMMATORY LANGUAGE: TURNING POISONS INTO HONEY

Our second conflict resolution format addresses the problematic and important topic of negative language. It is very easy for the conflict manager to get drawn into, or to be sidetracked by, the language of negativity and conflict that can so easily escalate a situation. The following format will help you both to avoid this pitfall and to redirect those in conflict towards a more productive form of expression of their differences.

The technique of reframing damaging, negative or poisonous language is one of the most valuable communication skills a manager can master. It is all about transforming strongly felt – but highly judgemental – comments that disparage or put people down into something more positive and constructive. This is done by leaving out the negative words and putting the emphasis on the issue they are concerned about.

Almost everyone wants people around them to *collude* with them when they are talking about their negative feelings about someone else. We want people to agree with us in our judgements about other people, no matter how true or untrue they might be. Now, in our personal life, it might be acceptable to collude and say, yes, so and so is awful, or agree with whatever is being said about them. But this is not acceptable or professional in our working lives – and can have damaging effects. To maintain professional standards we need to manage our communications positively by reflecting back or acknowledging what the critical person is saying whilst reframing the negative or derogatory aspects of what is being alleged.

When will you need to reframe negative language?

Transforming 'poison into honey' by reframing is relevant in a whole variety of work situations, including:

■ when you call in two or more members of staff into your office who are having difficulties working together;
■ when a member of your staff or a customer/client comes to you complaining about someone else;
■ when strong feelings or complaints arise between staff in a team meeting;
■ when someone is venting their criticisms of someone else;
■ when anyone is trying to pressurize you to accept or to act upon their viewpoint using emotionally charged or threatening language.

To be able to 'reframe negative language' competently and swiftly takes practice and a high level of professionalism and adeptness in communication. Where two people are engaged in dispute, your constructive summary of what each person says should both reflect the meaning for the speaker and, at the same time, be acceptable to the other person – a delicate balance.

There is a fine balance in how a manager can achieve this. If you neutralize your language too much, then the speaker may feel you have missed the meaning. In such cases, people will feel compelled to repeat the criticism because they will feel that you have not understood them. On the other hand, if your summary of what they are saying is too negative or critical, you will lose rapport with the person being criticized, who will feel you are taking sides. If this happens, that person in turn will be likely to react strongly and escalate the conflict.

The basic aim of the technique is to summarize the main issues in what someone is saying in such a way as to eliminate the negative, judgemental or irrelevant elements. It is a skill that is used all the time in mediation, and it is one that managers can incorporate as a valuable tool for everyday conflict management.

Practical examples of how to reframe inflammatory language

▌ Summarize briefly the key issues within what they are saying. There may be a number of issues present; listen out for them all and re-state each of them in your summary:

   Manager. *'So the issues for you are.../So the way you are seeing things.../ So in your perception.../So from your point of view...'*

▌ Eliminate blame, negativity or derogatory comments or opinions:

   Employee: *'Sarah must be stupid, I have told her to do the work in this particular way and she still hasn't done it!'*

   Manager: *'So you feel you have asked Sarah to work in a particular way and this has not happened.'*

▌ Use neutral language:

   E. *'He is an old, useless sexist manager and he calls me names like "sweetheart".'*

   M. *'You do not like the words your manager uses when he speaks to you – which you feel are sexist.'*

▌ Acknowledge and affirm feelings:

   E. *'What a stupid thing to say.'*

   M. *'You disagree with what she is saying.'*

▌ Change negatives into positives when you can (say what the person wants, rather than what s/he doesn't want):

   E. *'I am always doing all the hard work in our office and she is not pulling her weight.'*

   M. *'So you want the work load in your office to be distributed more equally,'*

   or *'So the issue for you is about how work is distributed.'*

■ Avoid judgemental comments but still get to the main issues:
  E. *'He is always late and doesn't care about the work.'*
  M. *'So, for you, the issue is about his time keeping and what you feel is his attitude to work.'*
■ Emphasize common ground:
  E. *'I can't believe that she is saying that about me – it's her who interrupts me all the time and has a go at me.'*
  M. *'So you both want to work and to communicate to each other in a more constructive way.'*
■ Emphasize the positive:
  E. *'She may have a point but I don't see why I should listen to her.'*
  M. *'So you can understand the point she is making.'*
■ Highlight any conciliatory gestures:
  M. *'You mentioned earlier that you may be willing to consider...'*
■ Add in feelings, if very strong:
  M. *'You seem particularly upset about...'*
  (Note: Adding in the words *'you feel'* helps put it back to the speaker as his or her own experience.)
■ Avoid taking sides:
  – by repeating any negative words or re-stating judgements;
  – by putting your own interpretation on what is being said;
  – by significantly changing the issues or the meaning.

Remember the purpose of your intervention, as a manager, is to encourage mutual understanding by clarifying the main issues involved and by helping people to move forwards. Reframing language can help you achieve understanding. *People may never reach agreement on what happened in the past, but you can help them move on and agree on solutions or changes in behaviour for the future.*

Watch your focus of attention

Finally beware where you put your attention. The elements that get your attention are the ones that will grow. If you put most of your attention and energy into the negatives of a complaint, then you will get more of that, you will evoke more of the negative, the blame and the put downs. If you can remain professional and calm and clearly state the actual *issues* involved (rather than engaging with belittling, provocative or tangential remarks), then you will be more likely to help people find *workable positive solutions*.

CHANGING AN IMPASSE INTO A WIN–WIN SOLUTION

One of the main theoretical aspects of mediation, the concept of win–win solutions (already discussed in Chapter 3) can come in very handy when you are managing people in an everyday work context. Have you ever been in a situation with colleagues, members of your staff or customer/clients when you get stuck in an argument or a negotiation and you feel they are just being belligerent and argumentative and will not budge an inch? Then this format is for you.

The concept of win–win negotiating is one of the underpinning concepts in mediation theory (Fisher, Ury and Patton, 1991) and can also be used by individuals or managers when in a situation of negotiation or dealing with differences of opinion or needs.

You want to find a solution but you do not want to just cave in and do whatever the other party demands. Neither do you want to just steamroll people and push them into doing just what you want, leaving them resentful and uncooperative (and risking the loss of a valuable client or supplier).

Basically win–win communication techniques are all about your using your brain and your skills to find ways in which you and the other person can both get your needs met. *This is about standing up for yourself and about standing up for the other person at the same time.*

If you can master this technique then you will be able to skilfully and smoothly turn an obstructive and potentially annoying situation into one of professional ease using solutions and strategies that keep everyone satisfied. And they probably will not even know how you do it. Quite understandably, it is very challenging when someone is making a demand or only wants their way, but the four steps of the technique will enable you to turn an 'impasse' situation around within minutes. The art of skilful win–win communication will be highly useful in many situations. Try the steps shown in the box on the next page and see.

RESOLVING EVERYDAY CONFLICTS QUICKLY WITH THE BRIEF MEDIATION™ MODEL

The Brief Mediation™ model is a conflict intervention approach specially developed by PMR for use by managers in resolving disagreements between staff or with customers. It is important that managers, or anyone

Four key ways to change an 'impasse' into a win–win solution

1. LISTEN

▌ Try not to react by getting defensive or annoyed.

▌ Listen carefully. What is the real issue or issues for the other person?

▌ Ask why s/he is acting in an obstructive way and not budging:

'Could you please tell me more about why you find it hard to move on this?'

2. TURN IT AROUND

▌ Show you are being reasonable and are open to finding a way forward.

▌ Make it clear that you will listen to their needs as well as stand firm on your own (or your organization's) needs:
'I want what is fair for both of us...'
'I would like to find a way that meets your needs as well as those of the company/this team/this department...'

▌ Turn the negatives into positives.

▌ Reframe unhelpful language into something more constructive and mutual:

'So what would work for you is... and, for my part, what I would need to see happen is...'

3. MAKE IT EASY FOR THEM TO SAY 'YES'

▌ Offer possible options.

▌ Say what you can do (rather than what you can't do).

▌ State any common ground or common goals you both share:

'We both want...' (and say whatever it is: the best for our client, to increase production in this department, to give the best possible service, to increase our quality/productivity/sales figures, to sort out this problem as quickly as possible).

▌ Allow them to save face, look for ways they can find an easy way out of the corner they may have got themselves in.

▌ Put your attention on solution finding and not on showing they are wrong or making them feel bad.

4. GO FOR THE WIN–WIN SOLUTION

▌ Reward cooperative behaviour, praise possible solutions they put forward:
'Thank you, that's a helpful suggestion.'

▌ Reiterate the solutions or positive ways forward you have found (and ignore tangential or unhelpful avenues).

▌ Be clear about those things that are 'non-negotiable':
'*Given that* this policy cannot be changed, what we could look at...'

▌ Clarify and re-state the details of the win–win solutions decided upon:
'So, what you're going to do is... and I will... Are we both agreed on this?'

whose role includes managing others, have a way of resolving conflicts or differences that is quick, effective and easy to use.

The model describes a form of conflict intervention that can be used for a wide variety of everyday conflicts or differences of opinion between staff or with customers or clients. It is essentially the use of a sequence of mediation skills that is particularly successful at directing and managing the communication between the parties in dispute so that they quickly come up with a solution that works for them. It is about being more flexible in the use of those mediation skills that can be effective for a whole range of everyday work difficulties no matter how large or how small. Most managers will never get the chance to be trained in and carry out a formal mediation, but they can use this informal, brief conflict intervention method for a whole range of difficult situations, conflicts, or strained discussions that they might face in their everyday work life.

Managers are usually very good at telling people what to do and at giving advice. This model has a different angle in that it encourages managers (where appropriate) to first use their communication skills to encourage people to find their own solutions, rather than jumping in and giving their own opinions or solutions.

Extending beyond the formal six-step model of mediation, into the use of the underlying skills in this way, brings mediation into the wider skill base of managers and enables its use by everyone within an organization for the smoother running of the business or service. This intervention is not a formal mediation and can be used flexibly. It does not require the use of the word 'mediation', there are no set ground rules and, at the end of the day, after first attempting to help people find their own way forwards, managers can choose to be more directive and add their own opinions or decisions as they think fit. Of course, for most of the time managers will be managing in the usual way, but these skills are a very useful part of their tool kit to be drawn upon when a situation requires it.

This Brief Mediation™ conflict intervention approach, with its clear focus on the issues and directing the communication towards workable agreements, can resolve many everyday conflicts in the workplace promptly and effectively. In sequence the Brief Mediation™ model is structured as outlined below.

INTERVENE

LISTEN AND SUMMARIZE

CLARIFY THE ISSUES

ENCOURAGE WIN–WIN SOLUTIONS

CONFIRM THE AGREEMENTS

Figure 13.1 The Brief Mediation™ model for managers
An effective and speedy conflict intervention approach for everyday work
conflicts or differences
© 2004 PMR Ltd

The Brief Mediation™ model

Intervene

First be aware, recognize that there is a problem or heated discussion
and find a way of intervening in a professional, non-biased way. This may
be on-the-spot in the office or in a meeting, or it may be that you will
need to invite those involved in the dispute to a private space or office.

As this is not a formal mediation, there is no 'contract' to mediate and
no ground rules. Intervene without making any pre-assumptions or pre-
judgements, and maintain a cordial, open-minded neutrality with a
stance of wanting to help or facilitate the situation.

Listen and summarize

Once you have found a way to enter the discussion or argument, direct
the communication so that both people say what they need to say in their
own words, one at a time. Listen and then summarize back in a brief
manner for each person – in a calm, easy way. There are many ways of
doing this, but one opening you could use is:

> I need to hear from each one of you, one at a time... Can you tell
> me from your perspective, what you think has been happening or
> what this disagreement is about?

Clarify the issues

Having listened to both, pull out the main issues or concerns between them, define them clearly and check your understanding:

> So, from what you have both said, there seem to be two main issues between you and these are... and... Is that right?

Encourage win–win solutions

Ask clarifying, open questions until mutually agreed solutions for each issue are found:

> So what needs to happen for this to be resolved between you?

It is best to deal with one issue at a time, otherwise the discussion can get confused and rambling. Focus on each issue and then discuss a solution for each of the issues that have been highlighted:

> Can you think of a solution that would work for you both?

Confirm the agreements

Once the agreements have been clarified, re-state them clearly, confirm the details of the agreements, check that they do in fact agree to them and thank them for their cooperation:

> So as I understand it, Fred you have agreed to... and Sally, you have agreed to... Is that right?

Chapter 13: The essentials

This chapter outlines innovative skills and formats for conflict managers to resolve everyday conflicts and difficulties in a quick and effective way.

It describes a whole range of valuable communication formats, including how to defuse angry situations, controlling your mind-talk, reframing inflammatory language, and changing an impasse or deadlock situation to one where both of you can win.

It also includes the special conflict intervention model for managers – the Brief Mediation™ model – for the quick and effective prevention or management of everyday conflict.

14
The philosophy of mediation and the business of empowerment

In Part III we have so far deepened our examination of conflict and outlined several practical formats that conflict managers can employ to help prevent or resolve emerging conflicts in the workplace. At this point we now extend our attention to the wider significance that mediation holds for positive organizational development and for the empowerment and deeper involvement of employees and teams in their shared enterprise.

We shall explore this organizational dimension in the next two chapters, beginning with the 21st century organizational 'identity crisis' and an examination of the contribution that the philosophy, culture and process of mediation can make to empowerment and to the sharing of control within the 'upended pyramid'.

'MAY YOU LIVE IN INTERESTING TIMES'

In many ways organizations can be said to be like people, in that they have their own personality and identity – of which they may or may not be conscious – that is clearly manifest in their corporate thinking, culture, interpersonal relationships and management style.

If organizations are like people, then we could perhaps talk of business and organizations in the 21st century currently undergoing something of an identity crisis. The essence of the dilemma and its history is summarized in the transitional model shown in Figure 14.1, which describes the 'upending of the pyramid' of command and control and the search, in modern times, for the Holy Grail of a differently configured and differently empowered business and organization.

This search is the product both of progressive organizational thinking and the pragmatic pressure on businesses to adapt and evolve in order to survive the cumulative demands of global markets, spiralling technology, multiple business alliances, stringent cost control and the new and continuously evolving commercial environments produced by the 'quality', 'continuous improvement', 'customer' and 'service' historical revolutions of the 20th and 21st centuries.

In summary then, the left-hand upright pyramid in the diagram reflects organizational structures and working relationships as they emerged from the industrial revolution. The right-hand inverted pyramid, by contrast, reflects the search in our times for radical alternatives of organizational structure and working relationships. It is essentially the contrasts and tensions between these two pyramidal realities that lie at the root of the present 'identity crisis' and that account for some of the conflicting experiments and fashions in the centralization and devolution of power.

Power, command and control in the left-hand pyramid of organizational structure and relationships resides clearly 'at the top'. The governing forces of capital, ownership and authority proceed 'downwards' only by permission or delegation from that point.

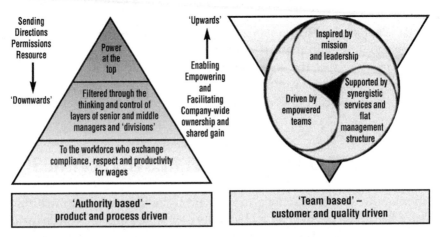

Figure 14.1 Upending the pyramid of organizational structure and working relationships
© MCRG 1995

The move from this first owner and authority-based industrial model towards the upended pyramid of democratic participation and synergistic design was precipitated through a series of historical revolutions in both society and in the marketplace. Working relationships developed significantly through social movements such as trade unionism and the emergence of the welfare state. Together with this social evolution came marketplace revolutions in quality, customer relations, cost control and globalization.

It is out of this progression that experiments in employee participation, continuous improvement, leadership and other alternative management styles have emerged, and these movements are summarized in the right-hand diagram by the inverted pyramid and the three-part 'drive wheel' of mission and leadership, synergistic flat structures with reduced management and empowered teams.

SO WHERE ARE ORGANIZATIONS HEADED IN THE 21ST CENTURY?

The social and political shift in the workplace power base that we have described has progressively rendered the command-and-control and authority-based model of working relationships less effective and, in our times, increasingly obsolete.

Gradually awareness has grown that the success or extinction of major modern enterprises – from small-scale operations to multinationals – has become dependent on the new and pressing criteria of power sharing, on the forging of reciprocal business alliances and on the primacy of service values and customer relationships.

Psychologists like McGregor, Argyris, Herzberg and Maslow variously explored motivational theory in the workplace, using models of 'self-actualization' and a 'hierarchy of needs' that posit human motivation not simply at the 'survival level' – of wages and personal gain – but within the 'further reaches of human nature' that encompass identity, creativity and self-fulfilment through work.

Organizational theorists like Likert offered frameworks for defining and operating these new workplace relationships as 'exploitative, benevolent, consultative and participative'. Other management theorists such as Drucker, Mintzberg, Schein and Elizabeth Moss Kanter offered rigorous and innovative analyses of the implications of this shift for management style and explored the organizational development and managerial skills needed to support the new 'psychological contract' in the 'post-entrepreneurial' corporation based upon 'empowered working relationships'.

In a nutshell, then, the re-engineered and upended pyramid of modern business and organizational life shown in our diagram, suggests that the Grail that business and organizations are currently seeking is to be found in an empowered and enabled workforce that is team-based, quality and customer-driven and in which power, resources, accountability and involvement are shared in a cross-functional and company-wide synergy.

Against this background the question that we will next consider is: 'what contribution can the philosophy, culture and processes associated with mediation make to this contemporary search for new and more effective dynamics and structures'?

MEDIATION AND THE BUSINESS OF EMPOWERMENT

Our analysis of the principles and process of workplace mediation suggests that the philosophy of mediation is clearly relevant to this organizational search for a greater sharing of power and control by those who actually create or deliver the product or service. When compared to standard business processes and working relationships the thinking and processes of mediation are unique and different in two major respects. First, the *locus of power* lies essentially with those who are directly involved because it is they who own both the definition of the problem and the means and control of the solution. Second, the *philosophical approach* that underpins mediation lies in the proposition that it is only mutually beneficial (win–win) outcomes that can ensure truly lasting gains and that will elicit the true involvement, responsibility and accountability that organizations increasingly need from their members.

Empowerment then is a central concept within the field of mediation:

> Empowerment describes the process of giving back to people control over their lives and work and the encouragement and confidence to participate in and take more responsibility for those decisions that directly affect them.

Empowerment in the organizational context also has significant new implications for the role and practice of management. It can be defined as creating an environment where others are equipped, enabled and encouraged to make decisions in autonomous ways and to feel that they are in control of the outcomes for which they have accepted responsibility (Heathfield, 2006; Page and Czuba, 1999; Honold, 1997). One striking example of such a genuine sharing of power and control by management is described by Ricardo Semler in his book *Maverick: The success story behind the world's most unusual workplace.*

Above all, employees must feel that they have the support of their managers to make empowered decisions. The idea of support highlights the difference between delegating and empowering. Delegating simply means giving someone a task to do. Empowering means that, with the responsibility, comes the freedom to choose the means of carrying out that task. It is a two-way interactive relationship, and for the manager it means moving from being a command and control 'boss' to becoming more of a managerial coach and the enabler and facilitator of the achievements of others.

EMPOWERMENT AND RESPONSIBILITY WITHIN MEDIATION

Empowerment is a core concept then within the philosophy of mediation and is one of the reasons that mediation has inspired so many people from different backgrounds and has been taken on board worldwide by so many different sectors. People are especially excited by the empowerment aspect of mediation, so it is worth outlining in more detail how this operates within our model of workplace mediation.

Empowerment rests firmly within the mediation process due to a number of factors:

■ The decision to resolve by mediation rests in the hands of those involved directly with the conflict or complaint because mediation is voluntary.
■ The content and the issues to be discussed within the mediation process are up to the mediation parties themselves.
■ The mediation agreements and solutions and the wording of these agreements are decided by the parties and no one else.
■ Adherence to these agreements is up to the parties themselves.
■ The mediator comes from a stance of positive encouragement and supportive validation for all the parties concerned that 'empowers' them and gives them confidence to move towards resolving even the most intractable issues and problems.
■ Experiencing the mediation process overall can empower people to resolve their difficulties and conflicts more directly and more successfully if they occur again in the future.

Of course, empowerment can be a double-edged sword in that it is a two-way process and involves joint responsibility. In mediation, employees may get the opportunity to retain more control over their dispute by choosing to mediate but, by doing so, they are also accepting more responsibility for their actions and for the restoration of performance. Such self-responsibility and empowerment is not an easy route for any of us.

This development of people's self esteem and confidence in their own abilities, however, links very closely with the concepts of the learning organization, of emotional intelligence and of a new style of 'relational management' called for in support of the sort of genuine empowerment that is demonstrated within mediation.

We have seen then that individual and group empowerment is inherent within the philosophy of mediation. We have also seen that the search for employee and team empowerment remains central to achieving flexible organizational structures involving the sharing of power, of control and of resources.

This common ground between mediation and business suggests that a valuable forum exists in which the philosophy, dynamics and skills of mediation can contribute significantly to the quest for greater sharing, responsibility and accountability in the workplace. We have briefly suggested here that the mediation movement may have much to bring to this dialogue, and in the concluding chapter we shall extend this discussion to consider how the processes of mediation can be employed to help create a 'co-entrepreneurial' culture and to generate mediated business solutions.

Chapter 14: The essentials

Organizations and businesses in the 21st century are increasingly looking to evolve and to restructure in ways that spread power and control across the enterprise. They need to do this because the top-down hierarchical cultures of command and control cannot deliver the degree of multi-functional involvement and flexibility needed to survive the pressures of the modern business environment.

The philosophy contained within the process and practice of mediation offers business and organizations a powerful model of empowerment.

Empowerment within businesses and organizations consists essentially of engaging everyone in the organization in the generation of the goals and means that will motivate everyone to deliver the desired shared gains in mutually beneficial ways.

The authors suggest that a valuable forum exists between the understanding and practice of empowerment that already exists in mediation and the contemporary search in business and organizations for the empowerment, involvement and accountability of employee and teams.

15

'Beyond mediation':
the culture of mediation and organizational development

In this concluding chapter we shall extend our 'forum' beyond the philosophical contribution of mediation to empowerment and consider next
the transfer value of the *culture and process of mediation* both to the development of *organizational cultures* and to practical ways of creating *'mediated business solutions'*.

MEDIATION AS A CULTURE AND THE 'CO-ENTREPRENEURIAL' BUSINESS

Organizational culture derives primarily from the nature and expression
of working relationships. Mediation for its part, as we have seen in
Chapter 12, operates from the attitude and life position described as 'I'm
OK – you're OK'. This governing attitude forms the basis of the respectful
and empowering relationship that is offered by the mediator and that the
mediator also encourages in those involved in mediation.

Viewing mediation as a 'culture' then suggests that a different 'style' of
organizational relationships is possible. Such relationships would invite
respect, mutual listening and sharing, and would involve all stakeholders in
the formulation of the mutually beneficial goals and in their achievement
through agreed means. Such a culture can be described as 'co-entrepreneur-

ial' and the supporting management and facilitation skills that such a relationship requires we will describe as 'relational management'.

Co-entrepreneurial, then, is used here to describe a relationship between management and their workforce that proceeds, as it does in mediation, from the co-ownership of power and control, and that results in:

- cooperative working relationships;
- continuously renewed working agreements;
- creative co-innovations and improvements;
- shared rewards based upon the results of the joint enterprise.

It is a relationship that is supported by the attitudes, stance and skills of relational management, which potentially provide the missing counterpart to the skills of performance management.

The facilitative and empowering counterpoint of relational management is necessary because the working relationship, unlike performance planning, is not a linear or logical phenomenon. Successful relationships involve understanding and reaching the 'whole person' and call for the skills of empathy, validation, exploration and facilitation that also lie at the heart of the practice of mediation. In recent years, management thinking has begun to recognize that the IQ needed to achieve clear outcomes-based planning and to deliver effective performance demands an equal and opposite complement of EQ, or the 'Emotional Quotient' (Goleman, 1995).

Like mediators, relational managers need to be able to elicit and to engage with the mental and emotional 'maps' of everyone with whom they work and deal. They need to be able to investigate and understand the subjective and personal beliefs, values, needs, emotions and behaviours that motivate and involve organizational members. Finally relational managers need to make the important attitudinal shift from the 'I'm OK – you're not OK' position (inherent in hierarchical command and control) to the 'I'm OK – you're OK' life position involving genuine respect, listening and enquiry in order to engage with their enormous potential for creative achievement.

If managers can experience both themselves and their employees as being 'OK' and make this belief the foundation of their working relationships, and the driving force of daily interactions, then the following exciting and transformational principles become possible within the workplace:

- All perceptions and viewpoints become potentially valuable and important and should therefore be heard and understood.
- All feelings are equally valid and are to be invited, respected and explored as a vital constituent of motivation and commitment.

- ▌ Creativity, planning, problem solving and self and team organization become equally shared resources and the expectation becomes that the business endeavour will grow in proportion to the numbers and diversity of those involved in the enterprise.
- ▌ Individual, team and group needs are seen as interdependent and hence equally important to business outcomes. These needs form the shared ground that will in turn be the seedbed for the shared gains that bring the lasting result for all those involved in the enterprise.
- ▌ Conflict of views, feelings, needs and outcomes are viewed as 'safe' and seen as the acceptable, or even welcome, starting places for sharing, learning, innovation, creativity and the rediscovery and redefinition of purpose, working relationships and shared gain for the enterprise.

In conclusion to this section, Table 15.1 shows in schematic form some of the possibilities – across the whole range of business and commercial relationships – that such a shift in corporate culture can achieve.

Where an organization, with and through its management, chooses to work from the premise 'I'm OK – You're OK' then it is not only opening up the way to maximizing creativity and output but also pre-empting conflict and preventing many of the current manifestations of organizational confusion and the frustration or breakdown of working relationships.

THE MEDIATION PROCESS AND 'MEDIATED BUSINESS SOLUTIONS'

In this chapter we began by suggesting that the philosophy and culture of mediation offers a style of working relationships that can take organizational development in the direction of new and valuable 'co-entrepreneurial' cultures supported by the skills of 'relational management'. Before closing our discussion on the implications of mediation for organizational development, we shall consider briefly how the very process of mediation itself can provide a powerful tool for the practical engineering of this 'co-entrepreneurial' business and organizational culture.

Gerard Fairtlough (2005) has established a very useful theoretical framework for defining and evaluating organizational style and effectiveness that provides a useful background to the processes that we are

Table 15.1 Comparative relationships and cultural effects of corporate 'life-positions'

In relation to	'Command and control' 'I'm ok – you're not ok'	'Co-entrepreneurial' 'I'm ok – you're ok'
Employee role	Specified by function, by job description and by directives from those in authority – sustained through performance monitoring.	Multi-functional roles, more fluid and dictated by the balance of business need and maximization of individual talent, skill and potential.
Authority	Driven by rank and power held by a small number of people who operate clearly 'top down' within strict parameters and permissions.	Based on cooperative and consensual decision making and driven by personal authority, by expertise and by business need rather than by rank or seniority.
Structure	'Hierarchical pyramid' and supporting multi-layers of management and bureaucracy.	'Flat' structure with very few management layers – operates with cross-functional teams and more direct decision making.
Executive power	Resides within layers of management and functional control and is clearly demarcated and prescribed.	Resides within the whole enterprise and is accessible to all based on needs and outcomes – often by team consensus.
Working relationships	'Dictatorial' or 'patriarchal' manager-to-employee relationships – 'Parent to Child' (may be 'critical or nurturing', see Chapter 12).	'Egalitarian' – equal and mutually respectful and creative relationships – 'Adult to Adult' (see exposition in Chapter 12).
Operating style	Business plan and strategy is dictated 'from the top' and governed by centralized policy and procedures; any clashes of functional interest are arbitrated by senior management.	Flat structures – favour 'bottom-up' planning, procedures and improvements. The enterprise is seeking 'synergistic' working with shared planning and operation in cross-functional teams.
Motivation	The employee is expected to be self-motivated but controls are applied through performance management monitoring and PRP.	Motivation tends to come from satisfaction, control over work, and due reward; also from values in the direction of 'self-actualization' through satisfying work.
Rewards	Tend to be allocated and proportional in line with authority, qualifications, role and seniority.	Tend to be allocated more equally and in relation to individual or team contributions and business results and profits.
Suppliers and co-producers	Will act from a position of dominance and dictate the terms, price and relationship.	View suppliers as allies and as sharing the collaboration and hence the profits.
Customers	Traditionally able to dictate to customers – but now risk losing markets and ignore customers at their peril.	The operation is 'customer-led' and the enterprise is engineered and positioned 'from the customer' back to the service delivery, design, marketing and production.

about to describe. In his brief but seminal work *Three Ways of Getting Things Done: Hierarchy, Heterarchy and Responsible Autonomy in Organizations,* Fairtlough claims that leadership in organizations comes not just from the top but 'from everywhere' and that it is simply 'hierarchy that stops it'.

Fairtlough's third significant 'way to get things done' he describes as 'responsible autonomy'. This is a simple concept but has revolutionary implications in that it describes a way of working in which 'a group of people with a purpose decide what to do, how to do it and assume responsibility for the outcome'. He writes:

> In this way, an individual or a group has autonomy to decide what to do, but is accountable for the outcome of the decision. It might be called 'no rule', or rather, no *external* rule. The existence of accountability distinguishes responsible autonomy from anarchy.

> (Fairtlough, 2005: 30)

This concept of 'responsible autonomy' describes in essence both the essential process of mediation and, by extension, the working processes of what we have called the 'co-entrepreneurial' organization.

The core process of mediation – as defined and analysed in Chapter 3 – contains within it all the essential ingredients both of Fairtlough's 'responsible autonomy' and of the democratic processes required to support the 'co-entrepreneurial' working culture. In detail, as we have seen, the mediation process operates from mutual respect and involves listening, the identification of interests, issues and needs and the negotiation and agreement of the best possible outcomes available that will benefit all parties involved in the venture. These essential ingredients to the mediation process provide a template for all that is practically required to achieve the democratic shift to the 'co-entrepreneurial' working culture in line with the working style that Fairtlough has described as 'responsible autonomy'.

Table 15.2 presents a very brief schematic example showing how this can happen and how the processes and the tools of mediation can actually be applied to create and sustain the 'co-entrepreneurial enterprise'. The table shows a sample of four key areas of business and organizational life namely: organizational change, innovation, conflict resolution and problem solving. To indicate the link with the process of mediation, these interventions have been termed 'Mediated Business Solutions'.

Table 15.2 'Mediated business solutions' for change management, continuous improvement and conflict resolution

There are numerous organizational development applications in which the principles of mediation can offer immediate new value and 'fit'. These include:

Management or development area	Involvement of appropriate personnel	Mediated processes	Monitoring measures and checks
Change	Stakeholders to be advertised and to 'self-select' as essential to or stakeholders in the strategic planning process.	1. Stakeholders to share 'maps', 'positions' and 'interests'. 2. To establish 'shared ground' and assess these against 'business needs'. 3. To create outcomes, strategies and action plans designed to deliver 'shared gain'. 4. These outcomes agreed by all stakeholders involved.	1. Assign monitoring roles and reporting. 2. Set up feedback channels. 3. Plan reviews, timings and fine-tuning mechanisms. As change rolls out, there may be a need to involve new parties and to repeat the process.
Innovation	Publicize the corporate innovations agenda and invite interested parties.	1. Stakeholders to share 'maps', 'positions' and 'interests'. 2. To establish 'shared ground' and assess 'business needs'. 3. To create innovative strategies and product or item action plans to deliver 'shared gain'.	1. Assign monitoring roles and reporting. 2. Set up feedback channels. 3. Plan reviews, timings and fine-tuning mechanisms.
Conflict resolution	Establish corporate channels to register the need to address any conflict issues. Set up internal and / or external mediators.	Deliver the six-step mediation process – beginning with individual meetings and progressing from positions, feelings and interests to establishing the issues and the shared ground, and generating creative solutions for agreement.	Return a copy of the signed voluntary agreements back to the commissioning agent in the business.
Problem solving	Publicize the problem agenda and invite those interested and involved to help generate solutions.	1. Problem solvers to share maps of expertise as well as any particular 'positions' and 'interests'. 2. To establish 'shared ground' and assess against 'business needs'. 3. To create innovative solutions with action plans to deliver 'shared gain' solutions.	1. Assign key roles, budgets and reporting. 2. Set up feedback and review channels. 3. Plan timings, monitoring and the feedback and fine-tuning mechanisms.

CONCLUSIONS: THE LAST WORD

One thing is for sure: mediation, as a dispute resolution process, with its associated principles and skills, is set for a rapid expansion in the UK as well as worldwide. Companies and organizations of all sizes and within all sectors will undoubtedly begin to look at ways they can incorporate and synthesize mediation within management or leadership training, change management processes, policies for resolving formal complaints and, last but not least, within aspirations and strategies for improving and changing the overall work culture of an organization.

This steady uptake of mediation will not just be about saving money and time. It will more likely strike home on the shop floor, in the office, in boardrooms as an approach that empowers and supports people to say 'I can do...' or 'I can sort it out' and 'I will find a way that truly meets my needs as well as yours'. This is not about pie in the sky; it is not about using mediation as another way of manipulating employees into giving more at their cost only.

This is a form of management, a way of managing relationships in the workplace that is based on the sound and sustainable principles of fairness, empowerment and respect: principles that will lead us into the 21st century and that will give us the strength and the sound ground to deal with enormous and rapid change in the world. This rapid change, the crises in our environment and the many differences and challenges we are bound to come across will demand the need for innovative and courageous ways of resolving conflicts between people throughout all businesses, organizations and countries in the world. Mediation is one of these ways – and it is a vital one.

'Bringing peace into the workplace' may sound a high ideal but one we would argue is a necessary one for all of us. Bringing 'kindness' or a certain compassion into the workplace, into working or business relations is also a value that underpins the word 'respect' and in all the ways we have detailed and outlined in this book that one can use to de-escalate aggression or stressful situations. People talk about the complaint culture; just maybe we can now begin to talk about the 'collaborative mediation culture'.

Mediation is a dispute methodology that is set to blossom and grow and is certainly here to stay.

Chapter 15: The essentials

Organizations going into the 21st century may need to consider different models of how businesses are run, how decisions are made and how the multiple layers of relationships between employees are handled more fairly. The older model of 'command and control' may need some radical overhauling towards encouraging employee participation, responsibility, collaborative decision-making and mutual, respectful working relations.

In terms of work culture, the approaches and skills inherent in mediation and conflict resolution point towards a different style of organizational relationships that can be described as 'co-entrepreneurial', and a different set of management skills that can be described as 'relational management'. Both of these concepts, which are important aspects of 'mediated business cultures', are essentially about moving more and more towards the 'I'm OK – You're OK' Adult base of work relationships.

The sound and sustainable mediation principles of fairness and respect will create the solid ground for the enormous and rapid change we are inevitably going to experience in our world. We have seen the proliferation and consequences of the 'complaint culture'; now we can set about encouraging and creating the 'collaborative mediation can-do culture' in a way that meets and rewards the real needs of all concerned.

Mediation is a new, innovative and courageous method of resolving interpersonal work disputes and differences. It has been taken up and supported by the UK government and many private and public businesses and organizations worldwide. It is presently going through its own rapid development, transmutation and growth and is certainly here to stay.

'Nothing makes us more unhappy than the untruth appearing as the truth'

Barry Long

The path to a world of peace must travel through the hearts of every one of us... compassion for yourself and for the other is the way... Dialogue is the most effective way of resolving conflict.

Dalai Lama

'The perfect way is only difficult for those who pick and choose.
Do not like, do not dislike; all will then be clear.
Make a hair breadth of difference and heaven and earth are set apart.
If you want the truth to stand clear before you, never be for or against.
The struggle between "for" and "against" is the mind's worst disease.'

Hsin Hsin Ming

'Stop fighting with existence, stop all conflict and the idea of being right... learn to surrender.'

Osho

Contacting the authors

Nora Doherty can be contacted through her PMR Ltd website at:
www.workplacemediation.co.uk
and by email at: pmr@workplacemediation.co.uk

Marcelas Guyler can be contacted through his website at:
www.mcrg.co.uk
and by email at: marcelas@mcrg.co.uk

Bibliography

Authors shown in bold are referred to in the text.

PART 1. MEDIATION

Acland, A (1990) *A Sudden Outbreak of Common Sense: Managing Conflict through Mediation*, Century Business

Beer, JE and Steif, E and Friends Conflict Resolution Programs (1997) *The Mediators Handbook*, New Society

Bowling, D and Hoffman, D (2003) *Bringing Peace into the Room*, Jossey-Bass / Wiley

Bush, RAB and **Folger**, JP (1994) *The Promise of Mediation: Responding to Conflict through Empowerment and Recognition*, Jossey-Bass

Carnevale, PJ and **Pruitt**, DG (1992) Negotiation and mediation, *Annual Review of Psychology*, 43, pp 531– 582

CIPD (2007) *Managing Conflict at Work*, CIPD

Deutsch, M and **Coleman**, PT (2000) *The Handbook of Conflict Resolution: Theory and Practice*, Jossey-Bass / Wiley

Doherty, N (1998) *Six-step Workplace Mediation Model and Brief Mediation Model for Managers*, PMR Ltd Training Manuals

Fisher, R and **Ury**, W (1981) _Getting to Yes: Negotiating Agreement Without Giving In_, Century Hutchinson

Herrman, MS (2006) _The Blackwell Handbook of Mediation: Bridging Theory, Research and Practice_, Blackwell

Kressel, K and **Pruitt**, DG (eds) (1989) _Mediation Research: The Process and Effectiveness of Third Party Intervention_, Jossey-Bass

Lacey, H (2000) _How to Resolve Conflict in the Workplace_, Gower

Lang, MD and Taylor, A (2003) _The Making of a Mediator: Developing Artistry in Practice_, Jossey-Bass/Wiley

Marick, F and Masters and Albright (2002) _The Complete Guide to Conflict Resolution in the Workplace_, Amacom

Mindell, A (1997) _Sitting in the Fire: Large Group Transformation through Diversity and Conflict_, Lao Tse Press

Moore, CW (2003) _The Mediation Process: Practical Strategies for Resolving Conflict_, Jossey-Bass

Moston, FS (2001) _Mediation Career Guide_, Jossey-Bass

Slaikeu, KA (1995) _When Push Comes to Shove: Practical Guide to Mediating Disputes_, John Wiley

Strasser, F and Randolph, P (2004) _Mediation: A Psychological Insight into Conflict Resolution_, Continuum International

Weeks, D (1994) _The Eight Essential Steps to Conflict Resolution_, Putnam

PART 2. CONFLICT RESOLUTION

Allport, GW (1954) _The Nature of Prejudice_, Anchor

Billig, M (1976) _The Social Psychology of Inter-group Relations_, Academic Press

Coser, LA (1976) _Continuities in the Study of Social Conflict_, Collier-Macmillan

Dalai Lama (2006) _Living Wisdom with His Holiness the Dalai Lama_, Sounds True

Dana, D (2001) _Conflict Resolution_, McGraw-Hill

Deutsch, M (1973) _The Resolution of Conflict: Constructive and Destructive Processes_, Yale University Press

Doise, W (1978) _Groups and Individuals_, Cambridge University Press

Donohue, WA and **Kolt,** R (1992) _Managing Interpersonal Conflict_, Sage

Fisher, RJ and **Brown,** S (1989) _Getting Together: Building a Relationship that Gets to Yes_, Century Hutchinson

Fisher, RJ, **Ury,** W and **Patton,** B (1991) _Getting to Yes: Negotiating Agreement Without Giving In_ (2nd edn), Penguin

Folger, JP and **Scott Poole**, M and **Stutman**, RK (1997) *Working through Conflict: Strategies for Relationships, Groups and Organisations*, Addison-Wesley

Hellinger, B, **Weber**, G and **Beaumont**, H (1998) *Loves Hidden Symmetry: What makes Love Work in Relationships*, Zeig, Tucker and Theisen

Kozan, M (1991, 1997) Culture and conflict management: a theoretical framework, Institute of Conflict Management 1997, **8** (4) pp 338–360; and in *Conflict Resolution Cross Cultural Perspectives*, ed K Avruch, PW Black and PW Scimecia, Greenwood Press, 1991

Mindell, A (2002) *The Deep Democracy of Open Forums: How to Transform Organizations into Communities: Practical Steps to Conflict Prevention and Resolution for the Family, Workplace and World*, Hampton Roads

Ruble, TL and **Thomas**, KW (1976) Support for a two-dimensional model of conflict behaviour, *Organisational Behaviour and Human Performance*, 16, pp 143–155

Salsberg, S (2004) *Loving Kindness: The Revolutionary Art of Happiness*, Shambhala Classics

Shenkar, O and **Ronen**, S (1987) The cultural context of negotiations, *Journal of Applied Behavioural Science*, **23** (2) p 263

Tajfel, H and **Turner**, J (1979) An integrative theory of inter-group conflict, in *The Social Psychology of Inter-group Relations*, ed WG Austin and S Worchel, pp 33–48, Brooks/Cole

Walton, RE (1981) *Interpersonal Peacemaking: Confrontations and Third Party Consultation*, Addison-Wesley

PART 3. CONFLICT MANAGEMENT SKILLS

Acland, A (1997, 2003) *Perfect People Skills*, Random House

Bandler, R and **Grinder**, J (1979) *Frogs into Princes: Neuro Linguistic Programming*, Real People Press

Bandler, R and **Grinder**, J (1981) *Reframing: Neuro-Linguistic Programming and the Transformation of Meaning*, Real People Press

Bolton, R (1986) *People Skills: How to Assert Yourself, Listen to Others, and Resolve Conflicts*, Prentice-Hall

Brinkman, R (1994) *Dealing with People You Can't Stand*, McGraw-Hill

Cooper, CL (ed) (1981) *Improving Interpersonal Relations*, Wildwood House

Crawley, J and Graham, K (2002) *Mediation for Managers*, Nicholas Brealey

Fensterheim, H and Baer, J (1975) *Don't say Yes when you want to say No*, Dell

Field, T (1996) *Bully in Sight*, Success Unlimited

Fisher, R and **Brown**, S (1989) *Getting Together: Building a Relationship that Gets to Yes*, Business Books Ltd

Goodman, AH (2005) *Basic Skills for the New Mediator*, Solomon Publications

Gordon, J (ed) (2003) *Pfeiffer's Classic Activities for Managing Conflict at Work*, Pfeiffer / Wiley

Hartley, M (2002) *Managing Anger at Work*, Sheldon

Hay, Julie (1993) *Working It Out at Work: Understanding Attitudes and Building Relationships*, Sherwood Publishing

Hay, Julie (1998) *Dealing with Difficult People*, Sherwood Publishing

Hay, Julie (1999) *Transformational Mentoring: Creating Alliances for Changing Organisational Cultures*, Sherwood Publishing

Knight, S (1995) *NLP at Work*, Nicolas Brealey

Kostere, KM and Malatesta, LK (1985) *Get the Results You Want: A Systematic Approach to NLP*, Metamorphous Press

Laborde, G (1987) *Influencing with Integrity*, Syntony Publishing

Laborde, G (1988) *Fine Tune Your Brain: When Everything's Going Right and What to Do When It Isn't...*, Syntony Publishing

Levi, D (2007) *Group Dynamics for Teams*, Sage

McDermott, I and O'Connor, J (1996) *Practical NLP for Managers*, Gower

O'Connor, J and Seymour, J (1990) *Introducing Neuro-Linguistic Programming*, Crucible

Rosenberg, Marshall B (1999, 2002) *Non Violent Communication*, Puddle Dancer Press

Smith, Manuel J (1975) *When I Say No I feel Guilty*, Bantam

Wagner, A (1981) *The Transactional Manager*, Prentice-Hall

Wilks, F (1998) *Intelligent Emotion: How to Succeed Through Transforming Your Feelings*, William Heinemann

PART 4. PSYCHOLOGICAL/ PHYSIOLOGICAL MODELS

Antonovsky, A (1987) *Unravelling the Mystery of Health: How People Manage Stress and Stay Well*, Jossey-Bass

Assagioli, R (1965) *Psychosynthesis*, Turnstone Press

Berne, E (1964) *Games People Play*, Grove Press

Berne, E (1972) *What Do You Say After You Say Hello?* Corgi

Berne, E (1975) *Transactional Analysis in Psychotherapy*, Grove Press (British Edition: 1975 / 1996 Souvenir Press)

Blake, RR and **Mouton**, JS (1964) *The Managerial Grid*, Gulf Publishing

Bradford, LP (ed) (1964) *T-Group Theory and Laboratory Method,* John Wiley

Briggs Myers, I, **McCauley,** MH, **Quenk,** NL and **Hammer,** AL (1998) *MBTI Manual* (3rd edn), Consulting Psychologists Press

Byron, K (1998) *Loving What Is,* Rider

Cialdini, RB (1998) *Influence: Science and Practice,* Harper Collins

Dilts, R (1990) *Changing Belief Systems with NLP,* Meta Publications

Goleman, D (1995) *Emotional Intelligence: Why It Can Matter More Than IQ,* Bantam

Greene, R and Elfers, J (1998) *The 48 Laws of Power,* Profile Books

Harris, TA (1967) *I'm OK – You're OK,* Avon Books

Harris, TA (1985) *Staying OK,* Pan

Huxley, LA (1963) *You Are Not the Target,* Wiltshire Book Company

Karpman, S (1968) Fairy tales and script drama analysis, *Transactional Analysis Bulletin,* **7** (26) pp 39–43

Lewin, K (1997) *Resolving Social Conflicts and Field Theory, in Social Science,* American Psychological Association

Long, B (1996) *Knowing Yourself: The True in the False,* Barry Long Books

Maltz, M (1960) *Psycho-Cybernetics,* Wiltshire Book Company

Maslow, A (1971) *The Farther Reaches of Human Nature,* Penguin Arkana

Osho (1995) *Meditation: The First and Last Freedom: A Practical Guide to Meditation,* Box Tree Ltd

Osho (1996) *The Book of Nothing: Discourses on Sosan's Verses on the Faith-Mind,* Tao Publishing

Rogers, CR (1970) *Carl Rogers on Encounter Groups,* Penguin

Rowan, J (1993) *Discovering your Sub-Personalities,* Routledge

Schutz, WC (1967) *Joy: Expanding Human Awareness,* Souvenir Press

Selye, H (1956) *The Stress of Life,* McGraw-Hill

Sternberg, EM (2000) *The Balance Within: The Science Connecting Health and Emotions,* Freeman

Stone, H and Winkelman, S (1989) *Embracing Ourselves: The Voice Dialogue Manual,* New World Library

Szasz, T (1997) *The Manufacture of Madness,* Syracuse University Press

Thomas, PG (1985) *Advanced Psycho Cybernetics and Psycho Feedback,* Classic Publishers

Tuckman, B (1965) Developmental sequence in small groups, *Psychological Bulletin,* 63, pp 384–399

Tuckman B and **Jensen** M (1977) Stages of small group development revisited, *Group and Organisational Studies,* 2, pp 419–427

Whitten, R and **Brown** K (1981) part of a presentation given at More To Life, London (formerly Life Training); these two authors created the term mind-talk

PART 5. ORGANIZATIONAL DIMENSIONS

Argyris, C (1965) *Organisation and Innovation,* Irwin
Barker, D (1980) *TA and Training: The Theory and Use of Transactional Analysis in Organizations,* Gower
Beer, S (1979) *Heart of the Enterprise,* John Wiley
Beer, S (1981) *Brain of the Firm,* John Wiley
Beer, S (1985) *Diagnosing the System for Organisations,* John Wiley
Bunker, BB and Alban, BT (1997) *Large Group Interventions: Engaging the Whole System for Rapid Change,* Jossey-Bass
Drucker, PF (1995) *Managing in a Time of Great Change,* Butterworth Heinemann
Fairtlough, G (2005) *The Three Ways of Getting Things Done: Hierarchy, Heterarchy and Responsible Autonomy in Organizations,* Triarchy Press
Fritz, R (1999) *Path of Least Resistance for Managers: Designing Organisations to Succeed,* Berrett-Koehler
Gibbons, M (2007) *Better Dispute Resolution: A Review of Employment Dispute Resolution in Great Britain,* Department of Trade and Industry
Guyler, MG (1996) *Internal Consultancy Skills for HR, Managers and Change Agents*
Guyler, MG (1998) *Partnership for Profitability for Allies and Supply Chain Partnerships*
Guyler, MG (2000) *Growing Teams: Team Facilitators Handbook*
Guyler, MG (2007) *Relational Management and the Co-entrepreneurial Business: Training Manuals,* MGC and The Human Business Limited
Handy, C (1989) *The Age of Unreason,* Business Books Ltd
Handy, C (1998) *The Hungry Spirit,* Hutchinson
Heathfield, SM (2006) *Employee Empowerment,* Human Resources, Aboutcom
Herzberg, F, **Mausner,** B and **Snyderman,** BB (1959) *The Motivation to Work,* John Wiley
Honold, L (1997) A review of the literature on employee empowerment, *Empowerment in Organizations* **5** (4), pp 202–212, from Emerald Journals: MCB University Press
Jaques, E and Clement, SD (1991) *Executive Leadership: A Practical Guide to Managing Complexity,* Cason Hall
Kanter, RM (1989) *When Giants Learn to Dance,* Simon and Schuster
Kennedy, C (1991) *Guide to the Management Gurus,* Business Books Ltd
Lickert, R (1976) *New Ways of Managing Conflict,* McGraw-Hill
Maslow, A (1998) *Maslow on Management,* John Wiley
McGregor, D (1960) *The Human Side of Enterprise,* McGraw-Hill

McMaster, MD (1986) *Performance Management: Creating the Conditions for Results*, Metamorphous Press

Mintzberg, H (1983) *Power in and around Organisations*, Prentice-Hall

Page, N and **Czuba**, CE (1999) Empowerment: What is it? *Journal of Extension*, **37** (5) (http://www.joe.org/)

Peters, T (1987) *Thriving on Chaos*, Pan

Schein, EH (1985) *Organisational Culture and Leadership*, Jossey-Bass

Semler, R (1993) *Maverick: The Success Story Behind the World's Most Unusual Workplace*, Warner

Semler, R (2003) *The Seven Day Weekend: Changing the Way We Work*, Penguin

Senge, P (1994) *The Fifth Discipline Field Book*, Nicolas Brealey

Shutz, W (1994) *The Human Element*, Jossey-Bass

Index

CPSIA information can be obtained at www.ICGtesting.com
Printed in the USA
BVOW06s1430250516

449540BV00010B/63/P